STEVEN HELLER

EURO

GRAPHIC DESIGN

AND LOUISE FILI

DECO

BETWEEN THE WARS

CHRONICLE BOOKS
SAN FRANCISCO

FOREWORD

Art Deco may have gone out of fashion, but it's not out of style. Introduced in the early twenties to insure French hegemony as the producer of postwar European decorative art and adopted by dozens of nations thereafter, this marriage of modern and modernistic continues to attract aficionados. Deco furniture, clothing, textiles, architecture, and graphics have incredible allure, and despite the political connotations addressed in sections of this book, Art Deco (or Art Moderne, as it was originally known) appeals to those who are drawn to the trappings of opulence, if only vicariously.

Nostalgia is what makes Art Deco so hypnotic and why curators celebrate it, revivalists pay homage to it, and dealers sell originals and knockoffs at exorbitant prices. However, while this may be the logical reason, it is not the entire story. In fact, it's unlikely that those who were alive in 1925 when Art Deco was introduced at the Paris *Exposition Internationale des Arts Décoratifs et Industriels Modernes* are the same ones who collect it today. Instead the ongoing heated romance with Art Deco is kept aflame by those who were born long after the style's demise when the privations of World War II put an end to all superfluous goods.

For contemporary Deco mavens, the style is so far removed from its original context that it is but a shell imbued with a mythic aura. Some believe Deco represents a bygone golden age when design and designers exercised power over culture and society, and so long to return to this moment in time. Others see Deco as a pure fantasy, a style without substance having little consequence in the real world. In truth both views are valid. Art Deco was indeed an elaborate marketing strategy conceived by impresarios and designers to induce consumers into buying fashionable and often unnecessary commodities and consumables. In this sense, Art Deco stimulated domestic and international trade in luxury goods, which affected the economies of many nations. It was also a superficial veneer designed to trigger desire as an end in itself.

Beginning in the late nineteenth century, the French, the world's major exporters of luxury, jealously guarded their precious stylistic innovations. But during the turbulent years before World War I, France's economy was threatened by formidable European competitors. Germany, Italy, and England, among others, had produced variants of late-nineteenth-century Art Nouveau and were furiously developing more modern stylistic wares. A plan was approved in 1912 for an epic trade exposition to be opened in 1915 that would showcase France's commercial assets, but the Great War postponed the event and forced a halt to commercial innovations of any kind. Following the armistice, the French government rescheduled the show hoping to reestablish its earlier status as a trade leader. Toward this end, industrial arts groups like the Societé des Artistes et Décorateurs encouraged French craftsmen and designers to engage in a novel way of creating decorative products, and they enforced rules that strictly governed conception and production. The most far-reaching of these dictates was the affirmation that no copies of historical models were allowed and only works of modern character were henceforth accepted as worthy of the French imprimatur. This regulatory decree, or "doctrinal aesthetic," is what gave rise to the formal Art Deco style.

Historical models were not, however, entirely ignored as long as they derived from far-flung antiquity, like Egyptian or Mayan sources. Deco also freely borrowed from Modern art movements and schools—Cubism, Futurism, Constructivism, Purism, and the Bauhaus—which provided myriad archetypes. Fernand Leger's Atelier Moderne, for example, was a wellspring of modernity that influenced certain aspects of Deco, as did works by the Russian avant gardists El Lissitzky and Rodchenko, the Dutch Van Doesburg, and the Hungarian Moholy Nagy. Nonetheless the radical essence of these avant gardes was somewhat threatening to bourgeois tastes, so Art Deco proposed an acceptable alternative. Rather than Modernism's austere geometric forms, the modernistic compromise proffered ornament based on geometric or cubistic patterns. Rather than Modernism's acute reductive ethos, the modernistic style proposed simplification that did not totally eradicate all superfluities. To the naked eye orthodox Modernism was too ascetic, so Deco applied splendid veneers that soothed bourgeois eyes.

Without the benefit of demographics or market-testing, Deco's impresarios astutely understood what the consumer wanted and how much the market could bare. Nonetheless Art Deco had its vehement detractors—classicists on one side and Moderns on the other—who argued that this *au courant* style was too eclectic, overly historicist, and downright mongrel. Such is the nature of being middle of the road—the fringes are unhappy while the majority is fed a diet of digested concepts and tested ideas. Yet as a style of compromise Deco was actually more expandable and inclusive than these other approaches. Classicism was locked in its prison of time, while Modernism existed behind a wall of dogma. Art Deco further proved adaptable in every cultural context and easily incorporated distinctive national traits. It could also be used as a stylistic code for two or more opposing political factions, like the Fascists in Italy and the Republicans in Spain, which both produced graphic propaganda in a heroic manner. Deco had no ideological loyalties, but it did represent a jaundiced view of the future, and therefore appealed to the forward-leaning youth culture of its time.

The Italians infused their Deco with Futurist typography combined with a Mediterranean color palette, which appealed to young rebels in the Fascist party. The Germans mixed pre–World War I *Sachplakat* (object poster style) with Expressionism during the years before the Nazis adopted a more turgid neo-Classicism as its national art style; the Dutch mixed rigidly geometric de Stijl with raucous Cubism for an eclectic modernistic appearance. And the Spanish and British each had distinct accents that built upon their respective national traditions and tastes. Shortly after 1925 Art Deco established itself as the dominant style throughout the industrialized consumer world because it appealed to both the affluent and bourgeois classes; eventually in a mutated form it trickled down to the working class, too.

Although the 1925 Paris exposition displayed a rather expensive array of merchandise, it also provided models at all marketing levels and ultimately made a tremendous impact on advertising—the industry whose mission it is to seduce the masses into consuming. One such proponent was the American advertising executive Earnest Elmo Calkins, who was so excited by the promotional innovations he found in Paris—from modish packages to posters to window displays—that he vowed to introduce a European aesthetic to the United States, which incidentally was not represented at the Paris event. Secretary of Commerce Herbert Hoover had not been unduly modest when he declined an official invitation to host a U.S. pavilion, declaring that American manufacturers had little to show for themselves. Calkins certainly agreed with this assessment. Yet he also believed that this design fête contained the secret of how to end America's inferiority. Deco was a means to goose manufacturers out of their complacency while enticing consumers to purchase goods more often and in greater quantities. Henceforth much of the advertising produced by his agency, Calkins and Holden, during the late twenties through the mid-thirties included Modern art (or at least the commercial equivalent) to inject fresh spirit into venerable products. He further introduced a unique strategy called "styling the goods" (which later became known as "forced obsolescence"), whereby advertisements, packages, and eventually certain products were regularly spruced up so that consumers could feel they were *au courant*.

But American advertising and marketing traditions did not radically change overnight. When the industry used avant garde conceits, the artistry was simply not as effective as it was in Europe. Despite the influence of the unique American Streamline style of the thirties (that culminated in the 1939 New York World's Fair, the most progressive and futuristic of any previous world's fair, as well as in the skyscraper style that produced such incredible Deco wonders as the Chrysler and Empire State Buildings), the American advertising industry was mired in antiquated graphic methods. Arguably, American advertising had long been word-based while European publicity relied on images. Ever since the widespread introduction of lithography (invented in Germany by Alois Senefelder) in the late eighteenth century, European illustrated periodicals and posters were the primary mass communications media. In the late nineteenth century colorful graphics and startling typography stood out on bustling city streets and boulevards, and as a result illustrators and poster artists were in great demand. Of course, this spurred competition among their agencies and studios, which in turn accelerated progress. Owing to the concurrent modern revolution in the plastic arts, European applied artists were even more motivated to push the boundaries of acceptability and taste.

But it was not as simple as turning a switch from old to new. Radical art did not immediately influence commerce because entrenched methods were defended and protected. Yet brand-new concepts of presentation gradually came about, in part, because many artists lead double lives—or did double duty—serving both a revolutionary muse and a malleable industry. Even before the 1925 exposition many of the leading Art Deco innovators were critically celebrated as "artists for industry." French, German, Italian, Spanish, English, and Dutch poster designers, many represented in this book, were courted by business to stylishly promote their wares, but they also gathered large followings of collectors and admirers. Today, the renowned Deco graphic works are every bit as indicative of the aesthetic spirit—a striving for originality *and* novelty—as are the clothes, ceramics, and chairs that took center stage in their time.

Yet posters are not the only graphic artifacts of lasting import. While they were the most visible images on display at the Paris exposition, they were not the only models of good graphic design. The leading French consumer magazines featuring posterlike covers, including *Le Monde Illustré, Femina, L'Illustration, Art et Décoration*, spread the Deco gospel. Just as ubiquitous were the point-of-purchase advertisements for the leading department stores as well as sundry and food packages for premium goods. These were permeated with the modern spirit. But what characterized that spirit? Arguably type was the most overt graphic element—even more so than illustration—that defined the Deco aesthetic.

Without emblematic typefaces Deco would not have had half its impact. As it was with the sinuous and curvaceous alphabets that symbolized Art Nouveau, rectilinear Deco typefaces were the glue that bound all the disparate moderne conceits together. In this role the leading French type foundry Deberny & Peignot was a wellspring.

Every nation that adopted Deco produced its own unique typefaces in its own type foundries, but many faces were modeled on Deberny & Peignot's inventions. In large part its aggressive salesmanship, including mammoth annual catalogs and eye-popping specimen sheets, catapulted Deberny & Peignot into prominence. While all type foundries issued reams of promotional materials, D&P's were the most superlative. Moreover, the foundry's signature typeface, Peignot, designed by A. M. Cassandre in 1937 and named after type impresario Charles Peignot, became one of the most emblematic faces of the late Deco period. This and other popular "hot metal" Deco typefaces, reproduced separately and on artifacts throughout this book, were readily available to advertising artists everywhere, giving them the opportunity to project contemporary auras for timely and fashionable products—further propagating the Deco style in the process. Today some of these typefaces are used in graphic design that evoke a nostalgic response while some have passed the test of time and remain current because they are viable and durable. Moreover, many of the posters, packages, displays, and magazine and book covers reproduced in this book are exemplary in any period. Take away the stylization and the basic design structures are strong.

But the goal of *Euro Deco: Graphic Design Between the Wars* is not only to preserve the treasures but to unearth the forgotten artifacts that comprise the critical mass of Art Deco graphics that dominated the print design milieu for almost two decades. Most of the examples reproduced here are comparably minor and were never intended to function for longer than the planned duration of a particular campaign—a few months to a year—much less stand tests of time. Yet even these lesser works are important links in studying stylistic evolution. To truly appreciate the range of Art Deco, and why it continues to be sought after and revived, it is helpful to see the diverse graphic products assembled on the following pages. Although not every piece conforms to the "high" Deco aesthetic of an A. M. Cassandre, Paul Colon, or E. McKnight Kauffer poster, all are imbued with traits that are decidedly indicative of time and place.

Connoisseurship, rather than analytic examination, is the driving principle behind the selections in this book. The authors, like many aficionados, have long been attracted by the sheer beauty of the Deco aesthetic, and have collected it for its inherent values as well as its historical importance as a source of graphic design. This intense interest on the authors' part should not, however, suggest that Deco is more important than other design styles and movements. It is certainly not as significant to the history of art or design as the heroic phase (during the twenties) of European Modernism. Paul Renner's Modern typeface, Futura, is much more functional than Peignot, and the clean and geometric Bauhaus page layouts of Laszlo Moholy Nagy and Herbert Bayer are more graceful than many of the excessively decorated Deco specimens in this book. Deco is not avant garde but draws from the vocabulary of new forms that Modern art and design introduced to the visual lexicon. Nonetheless, as a fingerprint of an era, Deco is just as important in the early twentieth century as other treasured stylistic manifestations are to earlier ages. Connoisseurs already acknowledge the value of Deco architecture, furniture, and clothing, so this book is a case for (and document of) the more ephemeral materials that characterize the style.

Finally, this book is a collection of six now out-of-print books from Chronicle's Deco Graphic Design series. The series had nine books in all, but the authors have selected six—*French Modern, Italian Art Deco, German Modern, British Modern, Dutch Modern,* and *Spanish Art Deco*—because they represent the most prodigious Deco cultures in Europe. We did not include *American Streamline* because, well, it is not European, although the design ethic reveals a European influence; *Japanese Modern* was left out for much the same reason; and *Deco Type,* one of our favorite books in the series, was eliminated because it covered a lot more than Europe, and typography is well represented in this volume. The books have also been condensed for this volume for reasons of both space and redundancy; approximately half of each original book is reproduced here. Each of the six "chapters" begins with a self-contained introduction that places the respective country's output in its historical context, and each thematic subsection (such as politics, industry, typography) includes a brief thematic précis.

Euro Deco celebrates a major stylistic achievement as represented by quotidian graphic design. Using this unique media perspective the book reveals the concerns of style-makers and -producers in their politically critical, culturally exuberant, and economically turbulent period between the two great wars of the twentieth century.

— Steven Heller

FRE
MOD

NCH
DERN

Early-twentieth-century Paris was a nexus of culture and commerce and a center for both modern painting and modern advertising. While painters altered the canvas, commercial artists popularized the avant-garde through ubiquitous bills and posters. Following France's victory in World War I, the public, eager to resume prewar consumption, was introduced to contemporary art forms through a plethora of advertisements for the *grands magasins* (department stores), automobiles, liquors, and cosmetics. French business and industry were the first in Europe to claim Modernisms, especially Cubism, as tools of *la publicité*, which led to a flurry of disparaging comments by orthodox Moderns such as Le Corbusier and Ozenfant, who charged that French advertising was "fake, marked-down" Cubism. Nevertheless, the public was made visually literate not by visiting Paris's great

INTRODUCTION

museums or galleries, but by strolling along its broad boulevards, where, during the 1920s and '30s, the billboards and kiosks were covered with pictorial iconography and decorative letterforms. "Advertising leads the public to acquire new tastes, just as it is led to buy products," wrote French graphic design critic A. Tolmer in *Modern Publicity* (1930). "The space allotted and the place held by advertisement display in our leading exhibitions of decorative art is, in itself, sufficient proof that advertising is definitely regarded as a branch of decorative art." Likewise, the leading Parisian poster artists A.M. Cassandre, Charles Loupot, Jean Carlu, and Paul Colin were recognized by business and public alike as cultural figures just as important in their métier as Picasso and Braque were in theirs.

French Modern graphic design was born in the *ateliers d'art*, or advertising departments, of the *grands magasins*—first in 1912 at the Printemps department store, and later at Galeries Lafayette, Bon Marché, and Louvre. "[They] wield in two directions," design critic Marcel Valotaire explained. "The first is their attractive window-dressing, and the second their system of catalogues which are sent out to the provinces each season." Like dimensional paintings, the window showcases combined fashion, interior, and graphic design into a Modernistic ensemble that influenced other graphic media. The catalogs were adorned with posterlike covers and filled with stylized, often geometric renderings of sleek models dressed in the modes then reigning in Paris. Through the confluence of advertising and the products being advertised, Paris quickly became the European wellspring of commercial modernity.

France built its economy on commercial Modernism. In contrast to Art Nouveau, which certainly had an impact on the Parisian cityscape but failed to achieve widespread public acceptance, Art Deco and its derivatives were ubiquitous in all forms, from buildings to matchboxes. In a nation that suffered the ravages of war, Art Deco came to symbolize not merely a return to prewar norms, but to postwar prosperity. And business was quick to realize that any tool that stimulated and increased consumption was worth encouraging. Advertising agencies, poster ateliers, and type shops grew furiously to meet the insatiable demands of business and industry.

The concurrent rise of industry and consumerism in post–World War I France demanded more from advertising on every level and provided the rationale progressive artists needed to defy the norms. In a challenge to the academic conventions of advertising art, the new *affichistes,* or poster-makers, influenced by modern art and machine-age aesthetics, rejected Romantic and ornamental rendering in favor of flat, constructed form. With

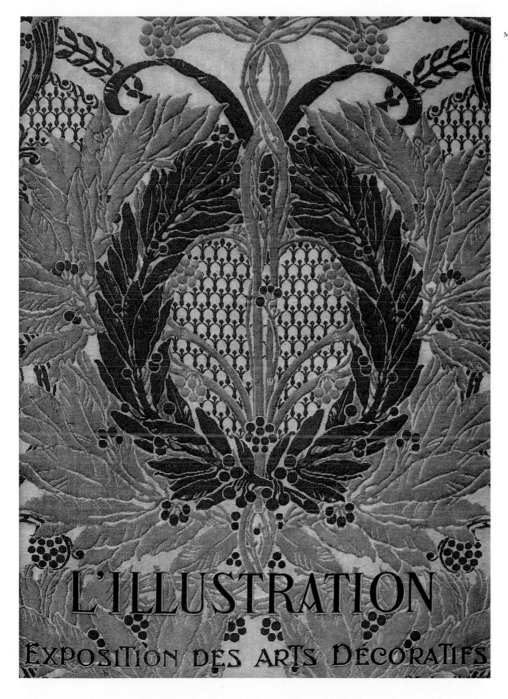

L'ILLUSTRATION
MAGAZINE COVER, 1925
ARTIST UNKNOWN

its foundation in geometry, the new poster was not loosely sketched or painted as before, but rather deliberately

built, as Cassandre described it, on a "precise architectural method." The style was characterized by fragmenta-

tion, abstraction, and overlapping imagery in keeping with Cubo-Futurist collage.

By 1925 avant-garde techniques had been adopted for their novelty, and in 1928 the editors of England's

leading advertising trade publication *Posters & Publicity: Fine Printing and Design "Commercial Art" Annual*

noted that arguments within professional circles about modern and nonmodern approaches had become as stale

as arguments between the Classical and Romantic schools. "If a design that takes some of the elements of mod-

ern art as a working basis accomplishes the end of selling goods, it accomplishes what is expected of it," the editors wrote. But they also claimed that in France, "artists follow too far their own individual path, that is, they tend to aim at purely aesthetic standards which are not necessarily good advertising." French *publicité* might have been more symbolically abstract than, say, realistic English or American advertising, but it did not require that the viewer strain in order to comprehend the message. And the innovators of French advertising art did fundamentally alter how messages were communicated. Through compositions inspired by contemporary painting rather than printers' layout manuals, products were not merely announced, but given auras that appealed to consumers at conscious and subconscious levels simultaneously.

Modern psychology taught advertisers the value of unlocking the subconscious, and modern art gave them the key. The audacious application of collage from Cubism, discordant typography from Futurism, and color-field abstraction from DeStijl captured viewer attention. Advertising pundits called the mnemonic image that prompted a kind of Pavlovian recognition "the fatal dart." The most memorable campaigns were the reductive ones that used a formidable design scheme to frame an unmistakable icon. "If painting has become simpler and more brutal, it is because a simple and brutal statement is at once formulated and understood more quickly. It is easy to see why publicity has borrowed from painting a mode of expression so suitable for its own needs," wrote A. Tolmer in *Mise en Page* (1931), the bible of French Modern layout. But if this statement appears to contradict the general perception of Art Deco as a fount of excessive ornamentation—the term *Art Deco* was coined in the 1960s to suggest the multifaceted style of the 1920s and '30s originally referred to as Moderne or Modernistic—it is important to understand that the French Modern graphic style between the world wars took many different forms. French Modern ran the stylistic gamut from the sumptuous ornamentation of high Deco's early Egyptian-Mayan hybrid neoclassicalism, to the brutal geometry of synthesized Cubism, to the spartan simplicity inspired by the Bauhaus and Purism.

Art Deco replaced the floriated madness known as Art Nouveau, which held sway for a brief period between the late nineteenth and early twentieth centuries. By the time Art Deco arose, Art Nouveau had devolved into a mélange of decorative eccentricities in which serpentine tendrils of stylized plants strangulated every designed object from furniture to jewelry to graphics. For some, the difference between the two styles was simply bad versus good taste; formally speaking, the fundamental shift was from curvilinear to rectilinear.

After the ostentatious artifice that preceded it, the straight line became the paradigm of beauty. Yet as in Art Nouveau, the ornamental motifs of early Art Deco were flowers, animals, and nymphs, as well as geometric patterns consisting of zigzags, chevrons, and lightning bolts. During this early phase, designers playfully borrowed ancient Egyptian, Mayan, and Oriental ornaments that were first introduced by Léon Bakst in his scenery and costumes for the influential Ballets Russes. The style appeared in the years before World War I, but was officially introduced seven years after the war's end, in April 1925, at the *Exposition des Arts Décoratifs et Industriels Modernes*, a world's fair of commercial products and style. In the *"pavillions de l'élégance,"* as the showrooms were described in *L'Illustration* magazine (August 8, 1925), France's leading retailers displayed furniture and fashions that marked the pinnacle of high Art Deco and Gallic eccentricity. But the *Exposition* also marked the thrust away from this elitist phase toward a mass-oriented one.

Decorative art had always been the prerogative of the rich, but in post–World War I Europe, the working and middle classes soon dictated their aesthetic needs, too. Modernists throughout Europe agreed that good design should be made available to everyone. And, depending on the social and political tenor of a particular nation, quality mass production was championed as a more-or-less inviolable right. But mass production requires standardization, and ornament was generally the first element to be sacrificed to the exigencies of production, both for functional and symbolic reasons.

Although the orthodox Modernists proffered a spartan functionalism that resulted in the elimination of bourgeois decorative excesses, most commercial designers without ideological leanings, especially in France, favored a reevaluation of form based on the dictates of the new era and opted for a middle ground which did not entirely eschew ornamentation. For the design of machines, appliances, and furniture, this meant conforming to, and building beauty into, the new industrial processes and coining a new ornamental vocabulary. For graphics, this meant complementing the industrial arts. This middle ground was best described by Marcel Valotaire, who said in "Continental Publicity" (*Commercial Art*, 1929) that to succeed, an advertisement must "give prominence to the product while practicing abstraction." This implied that graphic design should not be neutral, but should straddle the line between avant-garde and accessible. Ultimately, the public benefited from a revolution in design that did not so abruptly alter their tastes, but gave them a comfortable contemporary style that was of its time. "We find a growing demand for the new type of modern decorative art in all its varied forms," wrote Valotaire in "The Ateliers of the Grands Magasins of France" (*Commercial Art*, 1928). "It is the modern thing which sells nowadays."

French Modern graphics became the model for other European advertising, and some of the key artists exported their talents around the world. Within this milieu, type founding was another exportable industry. Although much of the lettering in Modern and Moderne posters was drawn by hand, the decorative styles introduced in this medium were in such demand that metal letterforms based on them were prodigiously produced. The poster became the testing ground for new lettering, and various foundries began to design, copy, and pirate original alphabets. None was more in the forefront than Fonderies Deberny & Peignot, which had marketed the most popular typefaces in all France, among them Nicolas Cochin, Moreau le Jeune, and Le Naudin. In the 1930s A. M. Cassandre added to this inventory when he designed Bifur, a unique display face that A. Tolmer called one of the "phenomena of advertising," and Peignot (after the foundry's proprietor, Charles

Peignot), which to this day is the quintessential Art Deco typeface. In addition, the French foundries produced sinuous decorative types that in America were dubbed "continental perfume faces" because they were used for that kind of advertising. Driven by market demands, the foundries issued lavish catalogs and specimen sheets, which increased business throughout the world and made French type both a popular export and the paradigm of Art Deco styling.

In 1932 A. Tolmer wrote in *Commercial Art* that French advertising was "advancing further and further beyond the 'easy,' the superficial, and the 'tricks,' which, though they gave the advertisement a certain spontaneous charm, were speedily revealed as tawdry by the facility with which they were acquired by artists of mediocre ability." This analysis of French Modern design is an apt introduction to the examples reproduced in this book. Some are what Tolmer might agree represent the epitome of French Modernism and Moderne styling, while others embody trendy "tricks" and novelties. It is not the purpose of this collection to distinguish between the high and low ends of graphic endeavor, but rather to exhibit the wide range of distinctive Art Deco methods used in posters, packages, point-of-purchase displays, labels, fans, magazines, and logos. Work by the leaders and the followers share the same stage as they did on the kiosks and countertops, in the publications and shop windows of France. Indeed, here the anonymous graphics are given even more prominence, for when presented in a collection these ephemeral works fuse into the quintessence of the French Modern style. This book is a celebration of what A. Tolmer referred to as the "miraculous originality of modern art" and of a period when French graphic design exerted a tremendous influence throughout the world.

Impressionistic poster graphics of the late nineteenth century celebrated and advertised popular culture. These posters became cultural artifacts, and by the early twentieth century advertising artists had been integrated into the cultural scene not as messengers, but as creators. A. Tolmer wrote effusively in *Mise en Page*: "It is curious to find that advertising should in text and style reveal an affinity with ancient art." Not only did Moderne approaches borrow from antiquity, but they were motivated by the ancient craftsman's creed. By the 1920s advertising art had become a full-fledged, respected, and sought-after profession. At the 1925 *Exposition des Arts Décoratifs et Industriels Modernes,* the graphic design of catalogs, posters, and lettering on pavilions contributed to the new cultural (and commercial) image that the French minister of commerce and industry wanted

C U L T U R E

to present to the world. The marriage of art and industry was key to France's emerging modernity; exhibitions and magazines made this clear to the public through symbolic motifs such as the metaphorical flowering of industry on the poster for the 1925 *Exposition,* designed by Charles Loupot. Graphic design was coming of age, which is why it is paradoxical that the final design for this poster was selected by a jury of architects, novelists, and politicians, without an advertising professional in the group. Nevertheless, 1925 marked the ascendancy of graphic design as a bona fide artistic métier. Comparing A.M. Cassandre and Loupot to the modern painting masters Picasso and Braque, A. Tolmer wrote, "the composition of a picture is nothing more or less than a layout." The modern spirit so pervaded French advertising that one commentator said that the "walls of the great city [of Paris are] a picture gallery whose publicity fires at the public at close range."

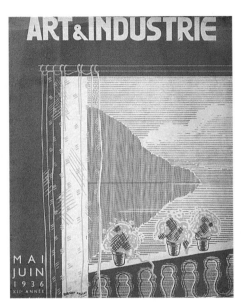

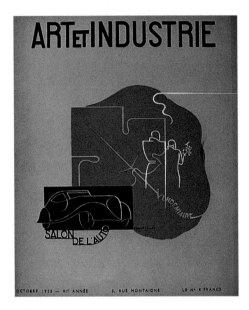

ART & INDUSTRIE

MAGAZINE COVER, 1935

ARTIST: ROBERT FALLOT

ART & INDUSTRIE

MAGAZINE COVER, 1936

ARTIST: ROBERT FALLOT

ART & INDUSTRIE

MAGAZINE COVER, 1935

ARTIST: ROBERT FALLOT

OPPOSITE:

EXPOSITION INTERNATIONALE

ARTS DÉCORATIFS &

INDUSTRIELS MODERNES

POSTER, 1925

ARTIST: CHARLES LOUPOT

MINISTÈRE DU COMMERCE ET DE L'INDUSTRIE

EXPOSITION
INTERNATIONALE
ARTS DÉCORATIFS
ET INDUSTRIELS MODERNES
AVRIL PARIS.1925 OCTOBRE

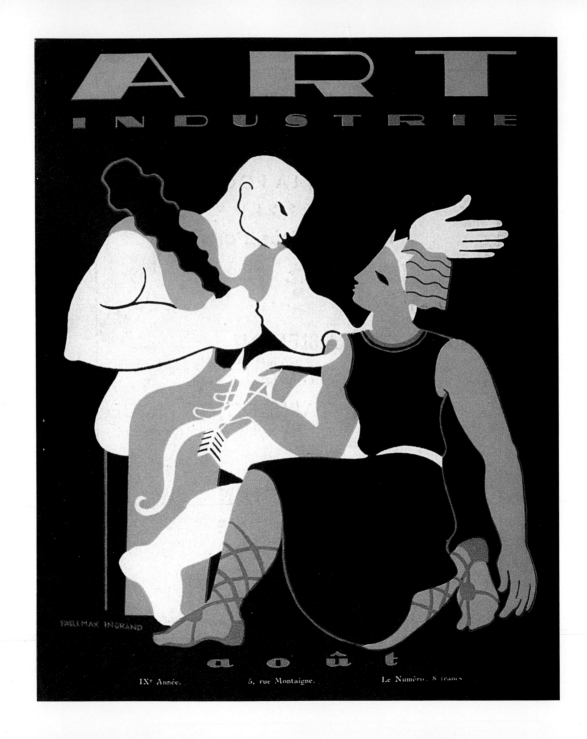

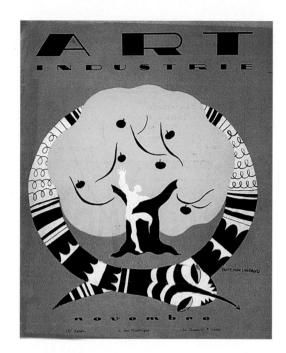

OPPOSITE:
ART & INDUSTRIE
MAGAZINE COVER, 1933
ARTIST: PAULE MAX INGRAND

ART & INDUSTRIE
MAGAZINE COVER, 1932
ARTIST: CHARLES LOUPOT

ART & INDUSTRIE
MAGAZINE COVER, 1933
ARTIST: PAULE MAX INGRAND

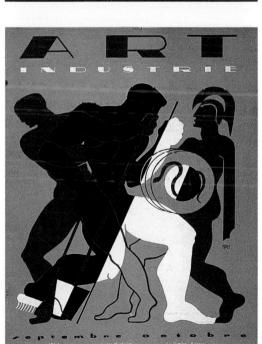

ART & INDUSTRIE
MAGAZINE COVER, 1933
ARTIST: PAULE MAX INGRAND

ART & INDUSTRIE
MAGAZINE COVER, 1934
ARTIST: C BÉNIGNI

LA DANSE

MAGAZINE COVER, 1924

ARTIST: MARIE VASSILICH

DUVAL / SVOBODA

POSTER, 1920

ARTIST: GEORGE BARBIER

PAPYRUS

MAGAZINE COVER, 1925

ARTIST UNKNOWN

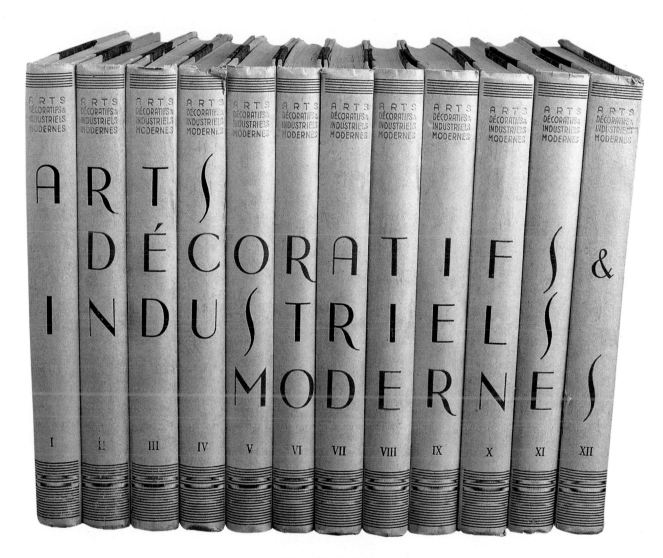

ARTS DÉCORATIFS &
INDUSTRIELS MODERNES
BOOK BINDINGS, 1925
DESIGNER UNKNOWN

The Paris collections are a seasonal rite that has only twice been interrupted by war. Between the world wars, Paris was the mecca for the great design talents, not the least of whom was Paul Poiret, the leading couturier who in 1911 founded the first modern design academy, *L'Ecole Martine,* and later introduced France to Cubistic trends in fashion. The Moderne style was sleek, supple, and sensual; its simplicity alone was a radical departure from the overwrought complexity of fin de siècle women's garments. Composed of few lines, the elegant contours of the new fashions were also so graphic that they influenced the Modern and Moderne graphic imagery which ultimately introduced fashion to the masses. The market for stylish, French, "off-the-rack" clothes continued to expand throughout the 1920s, and the *grands magasins* were quick to promote their well-

F A S H I O N

stocked emporia through seasonal catalogs featuring the latest zigzag, sawtooth, sun-ray, and rectilinear patterns printed against similarly geometric backgrounds. Graphic designers drunk with colors and shapes were given license to indulge in visual excess in the ways they framed and advertised the new. In September 1929 the editors of England's *Commercial Art* magazine characterized the exuberance of French fashion advertising this way: "The Frenchman takes his business as he takes his recreation, with a lighter heart than we do." And while most consumer nations—even those that had adopted Art Deco—were seriously developing marketing strategies, French graphic design, though no less committed to what marketers called "selling the goods," was also as playful as the market could tolerate and as outrageous as the public would accept. The confluence of a high Deco elegance and a mass-market wit made French fashion graphics the most enticing in the world.

GALERIES LAFAYETTE

ADVERTISING FANS, c.1929

ARTIST UNKNOWN

FEMINA

MAGAZINE COVER, 1926

ARTIST: GEORGES LEPAPE

OPPOSITE:

AU LOUVRE

CATALOG COVER, 1937

ARTIST: ALYANKI

AU LOUVRE

Grande Quinzaine
du 7 au 21 Janvier
1 9 3 7

37

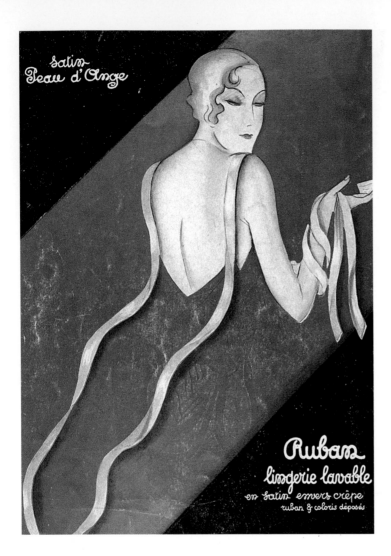

RUBAN

LINGERIE ADVERTISEMENT, c.1930

ARTIST UNKNOWN

PERUGIA

ADVERTISEMENT, 1932

ARTIST: PUBLICITÉ BARREAU

L'OFFICIEL

MAGAZINE COVER, 1931

ARTIST: JEAN DUNAND

L'OFFICIEL

MAGAZINE COVER, 1935

ARTIST: C. BÉNIGNI

L'OFFICIEL

MAGAZINE COVER, 1934

ARTIST: KISHING

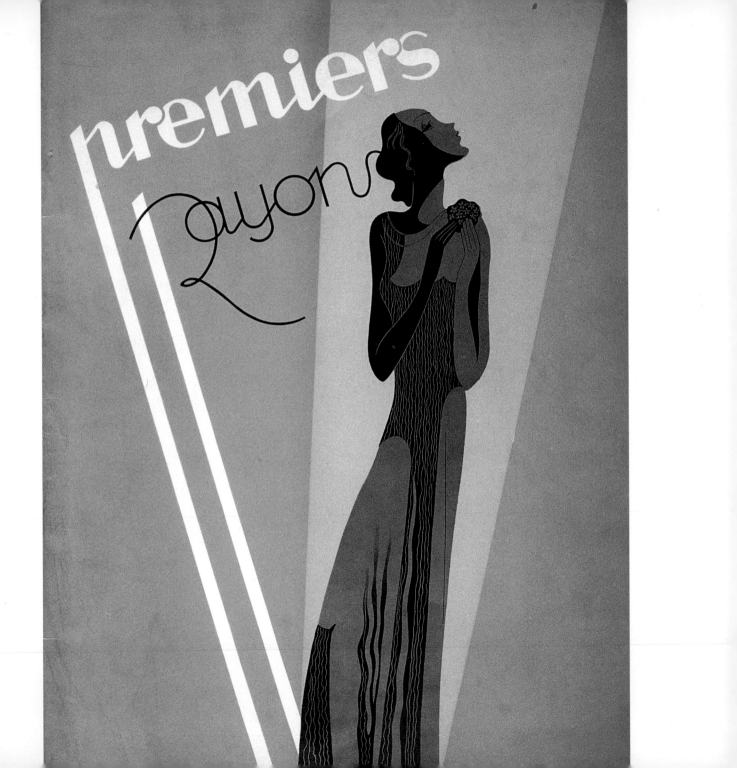

premiers Rayon

LA MAÎTRISE
ADVERTISING FAN, 1923
ARTIST UNKNOWN

GALERIES LAFAYETTE
ADVERTISING FAN, 1927
ARTIST UNKNOWN

OPPOSITE:
PREMIERS RAYONS
CATALOG COVER, 1931
ARTIST UNKNOWN

41

Fashion was the wellspring of French Modern graphic design, and it flowed over into the realms of cosmetics, fragrances, and sundries as well. Fashion advertising for the *grands magasins* was mythic, but the market necessitated that it also appeal to the real-life needs of the consumer. Not so in the area of beauty products. Cosmetics advertisements were based entirely on developing allures for various products that were more or less the same. To package, label, and promote soaps, creams, powders, shampoos, and perfumes, the leading manufacturers hired the services of ateliers where scores of anonymous decorative designers were employed. With the notable exception of posters, graphic design in this realm was reduced to the small-scale image, and designers were forced to use graphic motifs to immediately capture the customer's senses before the competition

BEAUTY

did. While ostensibly conforming to a Moderne style, many designs came close to echoing certain Art Nouveau conceits. Natural ornamental borders and background patterns were, for example, commonly used to give soap bars an enchanted aura. To complement such suggestive fragrance names as Soyons Discrets (Let's Be Discreet) and Un Rêve (A Dream), artists devised a repertoire of mysterious seers and stylized nymphs emerging from ornate frames. Packages for scented face powders were not mere boxes, but vessels of marvelous dusts designed to perpetuate youth. To be sure, everything was artifice, but it was so successful that France quickly became the leading European exporter of beauty products, and served as the model for how these products were packaged and sold throughout the world. French cosmetic packaging was Art Deco at its most neoclassical in its adaptation of antiquated artifacts, and its most contemporary in the creation of new decoration.

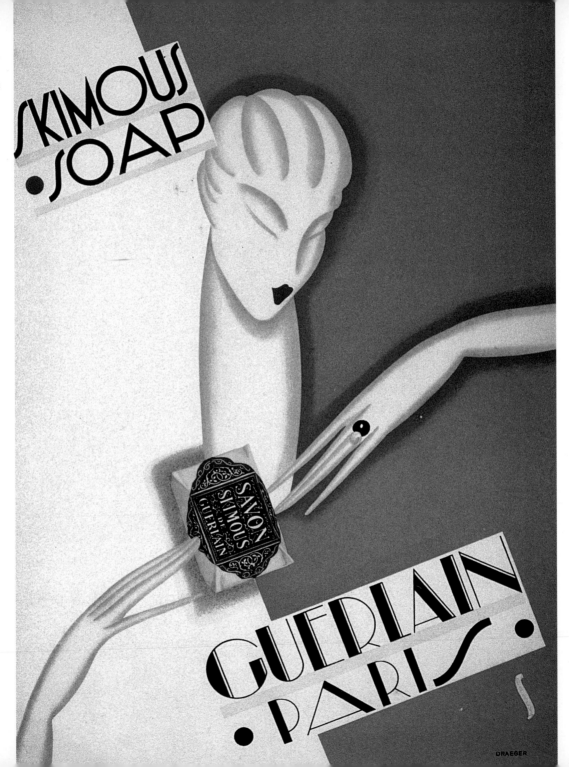

GUERLAIN PARIS
POSTER, c.1928
ARTIST: DRAEGER

SKIMOUS
·SOAP

SAVON
SKIMOUS
GUERLAIN

GUERLAIN
·PARIS·

DRAEGER

THRIDACE COSMYDOR
SOAP LABEL, c.1925
ARTIST UNKNOWN

LA VIOLETTE DE PARME
SOAP LABEL, c.1925
ARTIST UNKNOWN

COLD CREAM
SOAP LABEL, c.1925
ARTIST UNKNOWN

ROSE VÉRITÉ

FRAGRANCE LABEL, c.1927

ARTIST: R. DION

SOYONS DISCRETS

FRAGRANCE LABEL, c.1927

ARTIST: R. DION

UN RÊVE

FRAGRANCE LABEL, c.1927

ARTIST: R. DION

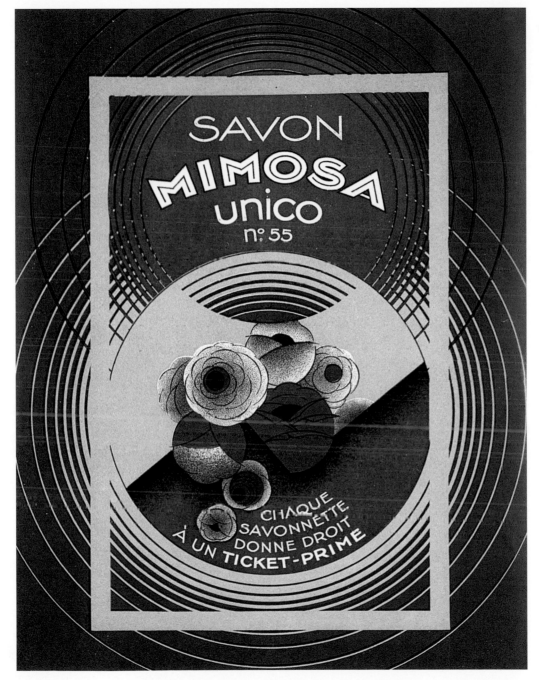

CAMELIA

POWDER BOX, c.1928

ARTIST UNKNOWN

RODOLL

POWDER BOX, c.1928

ARTIST UNKNOWN

GLYCÉOR

SOAP LABEL, c.1925

ARTIST UNKNOWN

GERALD

SOAP LABEL, c.1925

ARTIST UNKNOWN

CADOLIA

SOAP LABEL, c.1925

ARTIST UNKNOWN

MIEL RÉMY

SOAP LABEL, c.1925

ARTIST UNKNOWN

STADIUM

SOAP LABEL, c.1925

ARTIST UNKNOWN

L'INITIALE

POINT-OF-PURCHASE DISPLAY, c.1932

ARTIST UNKNOWN

LAVANDE

SOAP LABEL, c.1925

ARTIST UNKNOWN

LILIA

SOAP LABEL, c.1925

ARTIST UNKNOWN

LOTION "CAPPI"

COUNTER CARD, c.1928

ARTIST UNKNOWN

PERO

POWDER BOX, c.1928

ARTIST UNKNOWN

POUDRE MATITÉ

POWDER BOX, c.1928

ARTIST UNKNOWN

OPPOSITE:

TOKALON

POINT-OF-PURCHASE

DISPLAY, c.1930

DESIGNER UNKNOWN

L'ODALISQUE

SOAP LABEL, c.1925

ARTIST UKNOWN

les savons de toilette de la grande savonnerie de **l'Odalisque** 20, rue grignan Marseille

MONSAVON
ADVERTISEMENT,
1936
ARTISTS:
CHARLES LOUPOT
AND JEAN CARLU

ONDULO

SHAMPOO PACKAGE, c.1931

ARTIST UNKNOWN

SCHAMPOING MARCEL

SHAMPOO PACKAGE, c.1935

ARTIST UNKNOWN

POUR AVOIR DES CHEVEUX MAGNIFIQUES

DES
ONDULATIONS
MERVEILLEUSES
POUR CHEVEUX DE
TOUTES NUANCES
GRAS OU SECS
TEINTS OU NON

DE
FORMULE NOUVELLE
UNIQUEMENT COMPOSÉ
D'EXTRAITS TONIQUES
CONCENTRÉS et PRODUITS
NOUVEAUX, NATUREL
DE HAUTE CLASSE
SANS SAVON
NI MATIÈRE
NUISIBLE A LA CHEVELURE

essayez un

SCHAMPOING MARCEL
AUX EXTRAITS TONIQUES

COCKTAILS

The Moderne era is known for many things, not the least of which is cocktails. Few cities in the world are better known for ritual libations than Paris. It is no coincidence that the beverages and the words used to describe many of the world's most popular alcoholic drinks are French: liqueur, aperitif, cognac, champagne, and *vin (rouge et blanc)*. Like those of fashion and cosmetics, the wine and liquor industries during the 1920s and '30s were among France's most profitable. And, owing to great competition between brands, no expense was spared on advertising and promoting them. The leading artists were paid large sums to mythologize products with images that were historical, fanciful, and sensual. Like sports stadiums today, cafés and bars drowned in the logos of the leading sponsors, which were affixed to anything from napkins to umbrellas. In addition, fanciful

F O O D & D R I N K

posters and press advertisements featured witty mascots for leading brands such as Bonal, St. Raphaël, and Dubonnet. Consumers were treated to a plethora of premiums, including the ubiquitous advertising fan. This two-sided, hand-held mini-billboard featured a wide array of images designed to stimulate a ravenous thirst. Other foods and soft drinks were aggressively promoted as well. Enamel signs, point-of-purchase displays, and counter cards sold France's respective brands through stylized graphics that had appetite appeal and held artistic sway over the advertising culture. In addition to the elegant Moderne motifs, graphic humor was a powerful tool for transforming something such as a simple grain into a unique culinary experience. The package designs usually ignored the contents in favor of presenting graphic allure. Moderne typefaces, geometric patterns, and neoclassical motifs gave the product an aura as mythic as any fashion advertisement or cosmetic package.

BISCUITERIE PAUL
CANTREAU
PACKAGE, c.1930
DESIGNER UNKNOWN

MARRON CAO
PACKAGE, 1932
DESIGNER UNKNOWN

STELLO STANISLAS
PACKAGE, c.1935
DESIGNER UNKNOWN

TURPIN-MONOPOLE
ADVERTISING FAN, c.1928
IN THE STYLE OF LEAN & YLEN

BONAL
ADVERTISING FAN, c.1931
ARTIST UNKNOWN

BIÈRE DU FORT CARRÉ
ADVERTISING FAN, c.1925
ARTIST: ST. DIZIER

PIKINA
ADVERTISING FAN, c.1930
IN THE STYLE OF ANI LOSER

AMOURETTE
ADVERTISING FAN, c.1925
IN THE STYLE OF E.M. RAHUEL

LILET
ADVERTISING FAN, c.1925
DESIGNER UNKNOWN

BACOT
ADVERTISING FAN, c.1930
ARTIST UNKNOWN

CARCASSO OR-KINA
ADVERTISING FAN, c.1925
DESIGNER UNKNOWN

COGNAC SORIN
ADVERTISING FAN, c.1925
ARTIST UNKNOWN

UN BERGER
ADVERTISING FAN, c.1930
ARTIST UNKNOWN

SARETTE

PACKAGE, 1928

ARTIST UNKNOWN

CHOCOLAT LANVIN

PACKAGE, 1935

DESIGNER UNKNOWN

KOLA DE FRUTAS

LABEL, c.1925

ARTIST UNKNOWN

ST. RAPHAËL

TOY TRUCK, c.1925

ARTIST UNKNOWN

OPPOSITE:

QUINQUINA BOURIN

ADVERTISING FAN, c.1928

ARTIST UNKNOWN

The leading French poster artists owed a great debt to the painter Fernand Léger, whose canvases full of anonymous, Futuristic characters appear to have been created on a factory assembly line. The fragmentation and layering of images used in most Modern and Moderne graphics further symbolized the effect of the machine age on French art and society. Unlike the fin de siècle period of art, when advertising ignored the existence of the machine by masking it with floriated or fanciful decoration, the work of the leading French commercial artists interpreted, and even celebrated, a machine aesthetic both through abstract depictions of machines and the introduction of mythical machine-gods which embodied the new era. French Modern design never totally embraced the Italian Futurist's graphic obsession with speed, the American's adoption of the streamline veneer,

INDUSTRY

or other more radical machine age iconography, but it did not deny the new age. Instead, French graphics maintained a balance between Futuristic and nostalgic conceit. Typical imagery was forward-looking while firmly planted in the present. Dynamic typography—bold sans serif typefaces set in novel, asymmetric compositions—signified contemporaneity, while witty renderings of anthropomorphic machinery took the edge off of the imagery, preventing it from becoming too technological and mechanistic. French manufacturers went to great pains not to alienate their clientele by presenting overly avant-garde concepts, but they could not simply advertise such machine age wonders as furnaces, electrical items, or Pyrex pots and pans without introducing a degree of abstraction. Graphics for industry, therefore, relied on Moderne styling to capture attention, while giving the consuming public a more-or-less clear image of the product, designed to sell in the here and now.

ACIER

CATALOG COVER, 1937

ARTIST: A.M. CASSANDRE

CHAUFFAGE DEVILLE

POSTER, 1935

ARTIST: JEAN CARLU

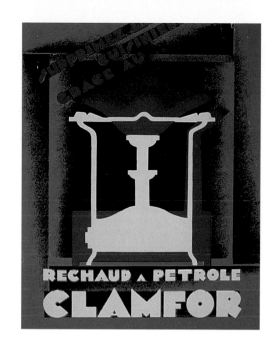

CLAMFOR

POSTER, c.1930

ARTIST: PATRICK

PRODUITS
CASINO

TUNGSRAM
POINT-OF-PURCHASE DISPLAY, c.1930
ARTIST UNKNOWN

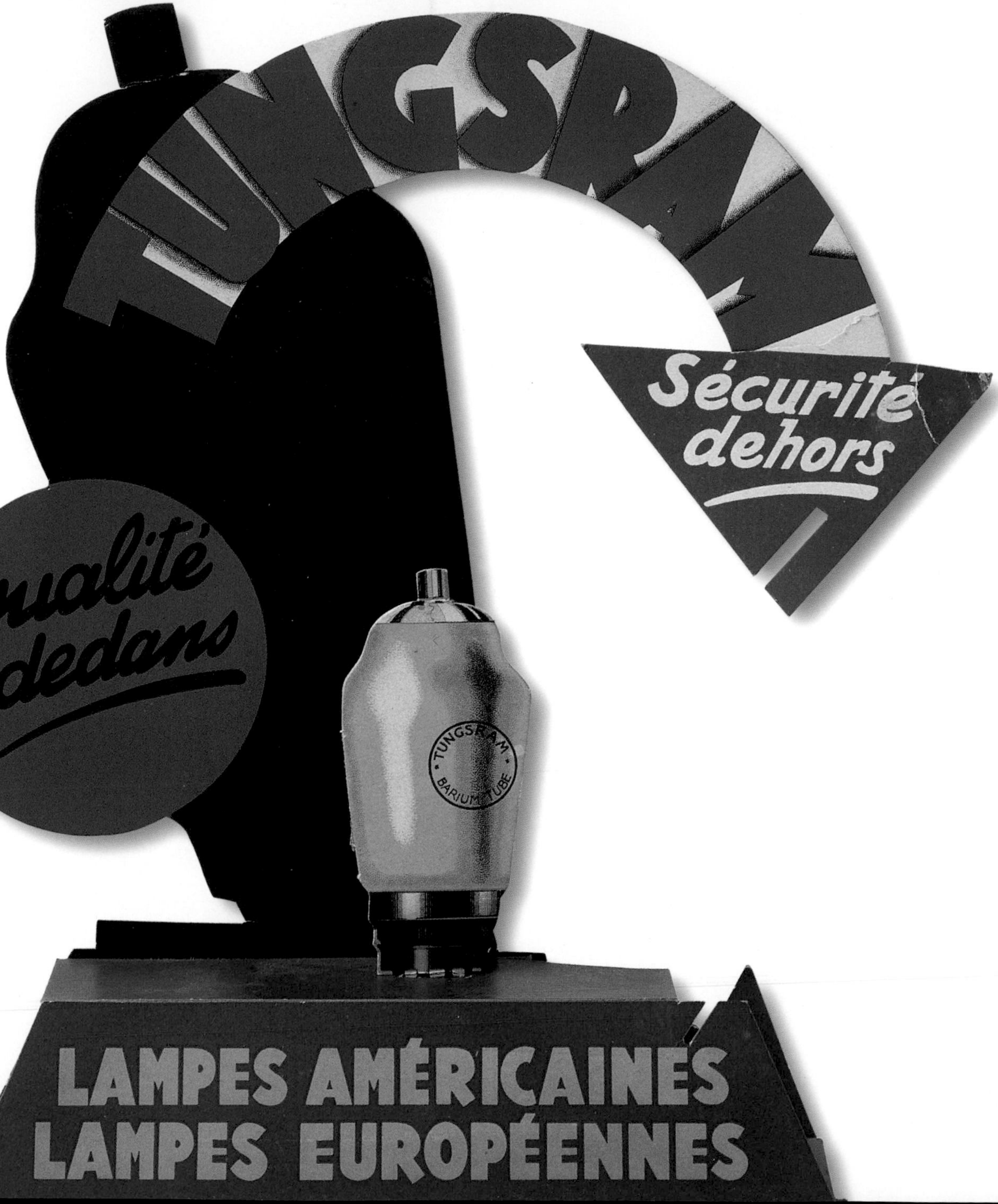

LA LAMPE
VISSEAUX
RADIO

TSF

MARQUE UN PROGRÈS

René Ravo

SATINÉE INTÉRIEUREMENT

MAZDA PERLE

N'EBLOUIT PAS

COMPAGNIE DES LAMPES

CHAMPSAY EDIT.

OPPOSITE:

VISSEAUX RADIO

COUNTER CARD, c.1928

ARTIST UNKNOWN

MAZDA PERLE

POSTER, c.1937

ARTIST: RENÉ RAVO

In the early 1920s French book typography was criticized for an adherence to convention that amounted to timidity. "Perhaps this monotony is a means of guaranteeing a settled habit of mind on the part of the reader," suggested A. Tolmer in *Mise en Page*. Real freedom in typography, however, could be found in advertising layouts, and particularly in modern posters where the letter was, in the words of A.M. Cassandre, "the leading actor." In the past, text was thoughtlessly added, but in the Modern French poster everything revolved around the word, resulting in integrated compositions of letter, text, and image. The letters were bold and geometric, and had a look unique to the age. Cassandre wrote that he was inclined "not toward a parody of inscription but toward a pure product of the T-square and compass, toward the primitive letter . . . the true letter that is sub-

TYPOGRAPHY

stantially monumental" (*A.M. Cassandre*, 1985). Since its inception in the days of Fournier and Didot, French typography has been known for its proportion and elegance, which continued through the modern era. Samuel Welo characterized these alphabets as having "grace and style, in other words the 'chic' so typical of the French people. It is not a letter for bold display but one that creates the atmosphere of refinement" (*Practical Lettering: Modern and Foreign*, 1930). The fount of type innovation was Fonderies Deberny & Peignot, which complemented a large catalog of traditional faces with some of the era's most novel and emblematic ones, including Bifur, Peignot, and Eclair. Through smartly designed tabular catalogs, specimen sheets, and the portfolio of design *Divertissements Typographiques*, and by employing the leaders in the field, Deberny & Peignot influenced a generation of practitioners in the ways of modern typesetting.

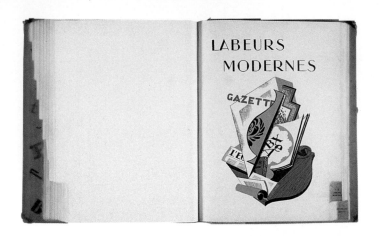

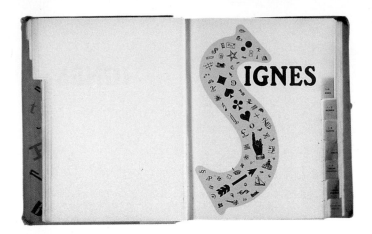

**FONDERIES DEBERNY
& PEIGNOT**
CATALOG, 1926
DESIGNER: MAXIMILIEN VOX

OPPOSITE:
PRÉSENTATION ETALAGES
CATALOG COVER, 1927
DESIGNER UNKNOWN

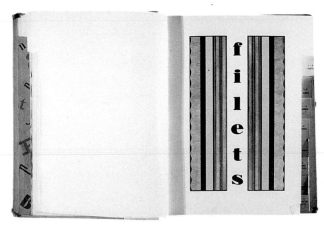

PRÉSENTATION
ÉTALAGES
MAGASINS
STANDS D'EXPOSITION
LE DÉCOR DE LA RUE
1927

LES ÉDITIONS DE "PARADE" 12, RUE GAILLON - PARIS

81

MILK BOTTLE CAPS

TYPE SHOP SAMPLES, c.1925

DESIGNERS UNKNOWN

DRESSOIR

ADVERTISING FAN, c.1923

DESIGNER UNKNOWN

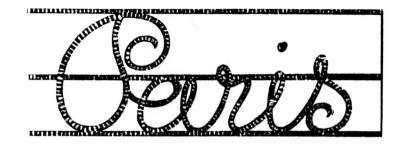

ALPHABETS ET
CHIFFRES MODERNES
TYPE SPECIMEN SHEET, 1927
DESIGNER: A. BARDI

ITAL
ART

IAN

DECO

Italy's applied graphic art of the twenties and thirties was exemplary in Europe for its persuasive power. A synthesis of avant garde and vernacular styles reflecting the political and cultural revolutions of the age, Italian graphic style was at once raucous and elegant. While it rejected a great artistic heritage, its roots dug deep into the past.

The *Risorgimento*, or second Italian renaissance, climaxed in 1861 when King Victor Emmanuel II, with the help of guerrilla leader Giuseppe Garibaldi, conquered and unified most of the Italian peninsula's independent city states. But even as Rome was not built in a day, Italy did not mature into statehood overnight. The trappings of nationalism developed slowly, as did an Italian graphic style, which, despite Italy's legacy as the cradle of European humanist art, took shape as a melange of foreign influences until the early twentieth century, when a national identity was forged out of modern art.

Italy's typographic heritage (the Roman letter, the model for the Western world's most significant typefaces, was originally derived from carved inscriptions on the Trajan column, A.D. 114) exerted little obvious influence on the direction of Italian graphic art and design during the late nineteenth century. Rather than build upon the classicism of fifteenth-century Venetian printers or the elegance of the eighteenth-century typographer Giambattista Bodoni, whose *Manuale Tipografico* (1788) was a guide to modern letterforms, Italian typographers and graphic artists turned their attention to French trends, like Post-Impressionism and Art Nouveau. The latter was known in Italy as Stile Liberty, and by the turn of the century this "floreated madness" had pervaded Italian design and architecture.

By the early twentieth century Milan was a crossroads of culture, commerce, and industry. Graphic artists from all over Europe traveled and worked there. Likewise, Italian artists visited the capitals of European modern art — Paris, Berlin, and Vienna — and carried home the Belle Epoch's most emblematic posters and periodicals. Europe's premier art, culture, and satire journals such as Munich's *Jugend* and *Simplicisimus* and London's *Studio* influenced a shift in Italian advertising art from nineteenth-century romantic illustration to twentieth-century objective imagery. These styles also were embraced in response to Italy's late change from an agrarian (and craft-oriented) economy to an industrial one, precipitating the development of commercial markets in Italy and abroad. Around 1900 "the first posters completely designed and composed by Italian artists appeared in Italy," wrote N. G. Fiumi, a critic for the English magazine *Commercial Art*. "It is, therefore, not [inappropriate] to say that Italy was one of the last important countries to make use of artistic advertisements." Italy's graphic artists borrowed visual languages as an expedient way to promote Italian products. Yet mimicking European styles was also a step toward developing an indigenous Italian one.

Among the progenitors of modern Italian graphic identity, Leopoldo Metlicovitz (1868–1944) and Adolfo Hohenstein (1854–unknown), both foreign

FIERA DI TRIPOLI
Advertising stamp for fair
1936

CATTOLICA
Advertisement for
summer resort, c. 1935

born Italians, became masters of the "new manifesti" with styles that drew upon lyrical heroism and organic decoration. As skilled realists they turned the commonplace into allegories: an automobile poster did not show a car but personified speed; a department store ad did not show a garment but celebrated universal beauty. Although their personal styles developed away from French Art Nouveau, they were nevertheless rooted in the aesthetics of the Belle Epoch. Conversely, one of Italy's early modern innovators, Leonetto Cappiello (1875–1942), assimilated his European influences (i.e., Cheret and Lautrec) so well that he might be considered *the* pioneer of an Italian style. Born in Livorno, Cappiello lived and worked in Paris where he mastered the revolutionary concepts of space and dynamic composition being introduced into French painting. An acerbic caricaturist, he manipulated comic figures that embodied the ideals or essence of a product. Equally influential was Marcello Dudovich (1878–1962) who, though born in Trieste, spent most of his working life in Milan where he practiced a type of Art Nouveau that combined exquisite draftsmanship with elegant styling. His posters of men and women in monumental poses bolstered the identities of such major Italian businesses as La Rinascente department store, Pirelli tires, and Borsalino hats. Another graphic artist of the twenties to contribute to the Italian identity, Marcello Nizzoli (1887–1967), was known for his classically inspired posters for Campari and others. About Nizzoli, N.G. Fuimi commented in *Commercial Art*, "I believe that the reasons for his success are to be found in the fact that he does not borrow from his contemporaries, but seeks all his inspiration from our great artists of the past, interpreting their aims with modern feeling."

This could be said about many of the leading names in Italian graphic art who reconciled their heritage with the modern. Not all Italian artists, however, were so responsive to their times. The movement known as "Novecento," which began after World War I under the influence of poet and would-be dictator Gabriele D'Annunzio (1863–1938), recalled the grandeur of ancient Rome in literature, painting, graphic art, and architecture. Novecento attempted to mythologize Italian history, and its exponents did succeed in creating a distinctly Italian design style by falsifying tradition. The result was pretentious art. Although Italian commercial art of the teens and early twenties was dominated by Stile Liberty and later Novecento, inventive practitioners tried the contemporary styles being unveiled throughout post-war Europe. The new graphic style known as Art Moderne (or Art Deco, a term coined in the sixties as a contraction of the 1925 Exposition Internationale des Arts Décoratifs et Industriels Modernes in Paris), is referred to by historian Bevis Hillier as "the last of the total styles." A broad-based aesthetic, Art Deco was a synthesis of ancient Greek, Egyptian, and Mayan decorative motifs, Cubist painting, and Machine Age symbols. After 1925 it became the dominant design trend in virtually all the industrialized nations as applied to a wide range of products and forms.

The Italian hybrid of Art Deco graphic design was the offspring of two

CATTOLICA
LA SPIAGGIA INTER-
NAZIONALE DELL'
ADRIATICO
Advertisement for
vacation resort, 1933
Erberto Carboni

CROCIERA AEREA
TRANSATLANTICA
ITALIA - BRASILE
Poster for airline, 1930

volatile parents: Futurism and Fascism — with consumerism serving as its stabilizing grandparent. Futurism, one of the twentieth century's earliest avant garde art movements, was founded in 1909 by F.T. Marinetti, a writer, poet, and painter, whose self-professed mission was to "challenge inertia" through perpetual disruption of the status quo. In poetry this meant replacing conventional verse with explosive rhythms and rhymes (in what he called *parole in liberta* or "words in freedom") that mimicked the sound of machines and weapons. In art this required destroying traditional notions of space and composition in order to express the dynamism of technology. And in typography this resulted in obliterating any semblance of classical symmetry on the printed page. "I am beginning a typographical revolution," wrote Marinetti in one of the movement's many hyperbolic manifestos. "My revolution is against the so called 'typographic harmony of the page,' which stands in direct opposition to the changes of style, moods, etc., which are typical of the style in which the page has been written. That is why we will use three or four different ink colors in the same page, and up to twenty different typefaces when needed." Many of the typefaces used were drawn from seventeenth-century specimen sheets, indicating that even the revolution in design could not be effected overnight.

Like the Futurists, the Italian Fascists were dedicated to violently attacking the ruling monarchy and bourgeoisie who, in the wake of World War I, were accused by nationalists of having sold out the nation to foreign powers. Both groups — Futurist and Fascist — were committed to social revolution and *Italianismo*. While Marinetti used art (often in concert with bombastic demonstrations) to propagate his vision, Benito Mussolini, a former socialist who switched allegiances to lead the Fascist party, used brute force in terrorizing his opponents. Though not always in agreement, Futurist and Fascist movements literally marched to the same drum in 1919 when they fought in the *Fasco di combattenti*, illegal paramilitary bands who fomented unrest.

The Fascist revolution succeeded without bloodshed when, in 1922, King Victor Emmanuel II succumbed to the threat of a Fascist march on Rome and invited Mussolini to become premier. Many Italians initially viewed Fascism as a first step towards ousting "old mummies and rotten figures," and so youthful Futurists threw their support behind the new regime by publicizing it in their periodicals, posters, and books. Marinetti held advertising in high regard, and saw its conventions as an effective way to propagate the Futurist faith, hence much of Futurism's early propaganda was presented in traditional formats. "Marinetti understood the power of advertising," wrote a critic, "which must reach people at every depth and height, excluding nobody from the social landscape." Futurists, however, took a more radical step: rather than products they sold ideas — an unprecedented use of advertising that required unprecedented approaches. Soon the Futurists began playing with graphic form. The results were anarchic compositions and symbolic letterforms.

GIORNATA DELL'ALA
Postcard for air show, 1931
Ver

Advertising techniques were adopted for use in other European avant garde movements during the 1920s. Dutch De Stijl, German Bauhaus and Dada, and Russian Constructivism all followed Marinetti's lead. All published self-promotional literature, designed books, and subsequently influenced radical changes in mainstream design practices. Nevertheless, these movements were kept out of the mainstream. The Constructivists played a role in the Soviet propaganda machine until they were superseded in the late 1920s by Stalin's Socialist Realism. The Futurists were favored as long as they concentrated on Mussolini's key objective, the creation of a Fascist image, but their vehement attacks on Italian traditions made them a thorn in the side of most Fascists, many of whom preferred Novecento. One member of the ruling council attacked them as "nothing but a group of poor little students [who] ran away from Jesuit school, who made some noise in the nearby woods and then had to be brought back home by [their] guardian."

TRIENNALE D'OLTREMARE
Poster for nationalist celebration, c. 1940
Cella

Despite the Futurists' devotion to industry, they were held in contempt by industrialists. With few exceptions, most Futurist advertising was used either as self-promotion or by adventuresome companies. "It is easy to imagine how the Futurists, considering themselves as the first and most audacious apologists of industrial society, must have encountered a certain frustration . . . for not having been fully used by the fields of applied arts and industry," wrote Claudia Salaris in *Il Futurismo e la Pubblicità* (Luptetti & Co., 1988). Indeed it was a struggle to convince business that these unprecedented approaches were advantageous. One supporter of Futurist design wrote about the need to influence Italian business this way: "It is necessary to force the industrialists to understand that a good poster and a good concept [must] generate . . . from the very modern brain of new men — everyone of them full of the dynamic and fast mechanism of our time, and capable of the most daring experiments of color and design." In the end, certain Futurist aesthetics were imitated by non-Futurist designers.

Image was the heart of Fascist politics, and graphic design was its backbone. Mussolini often became an art director when in detailed memoranda he criticized subordinates for their poor use of type or the placement of banners and posters. Yet in the early years of his regime he allowed artists leeway in the development of a Fascist style — hence the coexistence of Futuristic, Art Moderne, and Novecento approaches in art and architecture. "We must not take advantage of our heritage from the past," wrote Mussolini. "We must create a new heritage to be connected to the old one, creating a new art, an art of our times, a Fascist art." Ultimately, however, compromise came, at the expense of the avant garde when the dynamic aspects of Futurism were incorporated into an Italian Art Deco.

For a regime that promoted a cult of youth, the streamlined — or futuristic — aspects of Art Deco were the perfect vehicle for mythic depiction, and the airbrush was the best tool for achieving blemish-free effects. Art Deco expressed romanticism in its smooth surfaces and monumentalism in its rectilinear forms. Deco depictions of Fascist blackshirts made thugs look snappy and stylish. Even

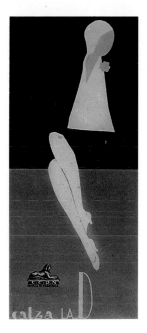

CALZA LA D
Poster for stockings, 1932

the *faces*, the charged emblem of the Fascist regime taken from ancient Roman iconography, was often streamlined through Art Deco conceit to symbolize the futuristic ideals of the party.

Italian Art Deco was not only manifest in political imagery but was propagated through design and printing trade journals and exhibitions aimed at designers working for industry and commerce. In the late twenties the Futurists did their best to influence these designers through manifestos like "Futurism and Advertising" (1932), by Fortunato Depero (1892–1960), Futurism's most dedicated advertising designer, who asserted that "the art of the future will be mainly advertising." Ambitious exhibitions of publicity were common; at the 1928 Futurist Festival, Enrico Prampolini designed an advertising pavilion. Other periodicals used to propagate modernity included Milan's *L'Ufficio Moderno – La Pubblicità*, which critiqued the latest design trends. *Graphicus*, published in Turin at the same time, was moderately progressive in its attempts to reconcile the Modern and modernistic. Beginning in 1937 the Fascist Syndicate for Advertising published *La Pubblicità d'Italia*, which set standards that indicated a preference for the modernistic over the Modern, but gradually programmed a stylistic shift toward Fascist realism. In contrast to official Fascist preferences, *Campo Grafico*, a decidedly progressive technical review, started in 1933, was rooted in Bauhaus principles and proffered a distinctly rationalist method (marking the ascendancy of the graphic designer over the painter) that became dominant after World War II.

Campo Grafico promoted a canon of composition consistent with the New Typography and "a mechanical art for a mechanical age" (i.e., photographs should replace painting), but action was taken by only a few intrepid designers, most notably in the layouts of the architecture magazine *Casabella*, or practiced by the members of Milan's Studio Boggeri. By the mid-thirties, mainstream Italian graphic design was ostensibly modernistic; it remained image-oriented and display types influenced by Futurism were common, including hand-drawn letterforms that accentuated the improvisational.

The evolution of Italian Art Deco from Futurism and Art Moderne took a decade or so to achieve, reaching its peak around 1939 when the demands of Mussolini's imperialism and the looming war forced a shift in design policy to decidedly unambiguous propaganda. Art Deco, perfect in peacetime for lulling Italians into a false security, and into accepting Fascism as a benevolent regime, was inappropriate when Mussolini demanded sacrifice and discipline.

From the beginning the Nazis forced all German artists to conform to rigid National Socialist standards, while the Fascists tolerated design pluralism as long as the symbols of the regime were not violated. What distinguishes Italian graphic design between the wars from other totalitarian countries was a modicum of individuality. In the final analysis, Italian Art Deco — futuristic and raucous, classic and monumental, humorous and hyperbolic — represented the spirit of the era, and all its contradictions.

FIERA DI VIENNA
Advertising stamp for fair
1936

**PROPAGANDA
ANTITUBERCOLARE**
Poster for tuberculosis
prevention, c. 1934
Lutin

The radical agendas of Constructivism and the Bauhaus caused Stalin to end one and Hitler to close the other. Mussolini did not suppress the Futurists but reconciled the needs of his regime with their value as visual propagandists able to synthesize the avant garde and modernistic. In 1923 he wrote, "I don't want to encourage anything that can be similar to an 'Art of the State.'" Nevertheless he understood that a Fascist identity combining classicism and modernism would appeal to old and young; especially the youths at whom Fascist mythology was directed. Mussolini wanted a Fascist image that reflected Roman glory yet symbolized the future. "He grasped intuitively that an image is built from the bottom up," writes historian Gian Poalo Ceserani, "by what happens on a day-to-day basis — with the road signs, the buildings, and emblems." In 1921 thirty percent of all Italians were illiterate, and graphic images were the most effective way of addressing them. Mussolini saw Italians as "political consumers," and as Fascism's "creative director" he controlled their behavior through slogans and symbols.

IL LIBRO DELLA IIᴬ CLASSE
Textbook cover, 1932
Mario Pompei

QUADERNO
Notebook cover, c. 1939
A. Rigorini

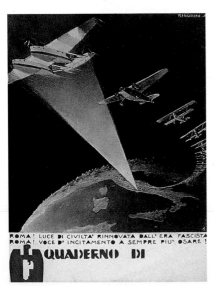

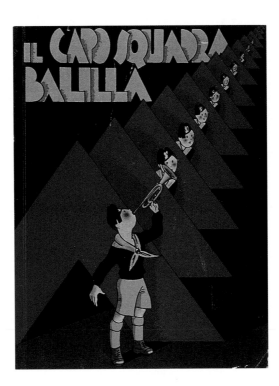

IL CAPO SQUADRA BALILLA
Cover for Fascist youth handbook, 1935
Zedda

STORIA E GEOGRAFIA
Textbook cover, 1933

LETTURE CLASSE SECONDA
Textbook cover, 1932
Angelo Della Torre

MACEDONIA
EXTRA

"La sigaretta di gran classe, squisita miscela di tabacchi orientali"

MONOPOLIO ITALIANO

10 SIGARETTE
MACEDONIA

MACEDONIA
Cigarette advertisement,
c. 1935

fascio

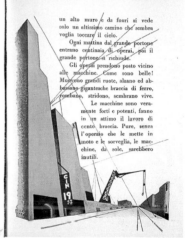

L'OFFICINA

COSA FATTA

CAPO HA

ROMA

ALLA A - DELLA Z
Textbook pages, 1935
C.V. Testi

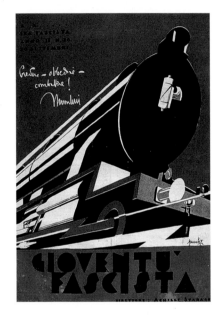

GIOVENTÙ FASCISTA
Magazine cover, 1932

GIOVENTÙ FASCISTA
Magazine cover, 1931
Cesare Gobbo

GIOVENTÙ FASCISTA
Magazine cover, 1932

GIOVENTÙ FASCISTA
Magazine cover, 1931
Cesare Gobbo

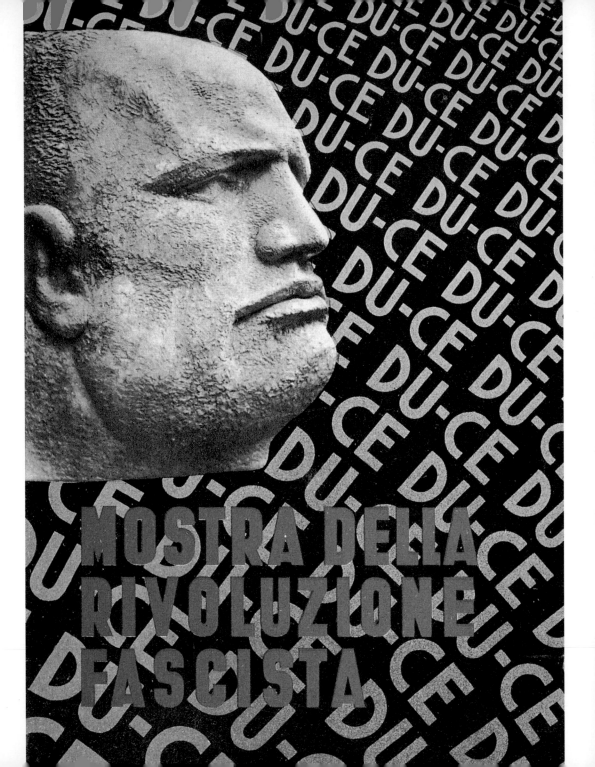

BONIFICA INTEGRALE
Book illustration, 1932
A. Calzavara

CONTRO LA TUBERCOLOSI
Diploma, c. 1938
Giuseppe Latini

OPERA BALILLA
Report card, 1944

**RICOSTRUZIONI
ZONE DI GUERRA**
Book illustration, 1933
A. Calzavara

**MOSTRA DELLA
RIVOLUZIONE FASCISTA**
Exhibition poster, 1933
C.V. Testi

MOSTRA NAZIONALE DEL GRANO
Exhibition poster, 1932
Marcello Nizzoli

Italian culture between the wars was not rooted in the artistic heritage of humanist art and architecture from the Renaissance, but developed out of twentieth-century rebellion. Throughout Europe modernist vanguards were attacking archaic political, social, and cultural institutions. No movement was more fervent than the Italian Futurists and their attacks on timeworn ideas. Speed symbolized progress; and the engine became the icon of rebirth. The Futurists devised new images and graphic forms to represent a cultural vision that was inextricably wed to their social one. Marinetti believed in "life as art," the total integration of day-to-day reality and the creative process. Hierarchies imposed by the old cultural elite, targeted for destruction, were to be replaced by social equality: "To communicate [efficiently] it is necessary to talk to the masses, not just the individual." This maxim, promoted in the "Futurist Reconstruction of the Universe" (1932) was perpetuated in periodicals. Yet despite their sincere attempts, what the Futurists called mass art was not necessarily consistent with what the masses needed or wanted.

NUOVO TEATRO
FUTURISTA
Theater poster, 1924
Fortunato Depero

**MARINETTI: PAROLE
IN LIBERTÀ FUTURISTE**
Book cover and inside pages, 1932
Tulia D'Albisola

TULIO D'ALBISOLA
Book cover and inside pages, 1934
Bruno Munari

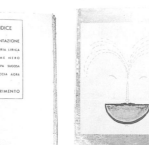

MODERNISSIMA
Catalog cover, 1920
Marcello Nizzoli

ASSOC. UNIVERSITARIA PARMENSE
Calendar, 1926
Erberto Carboni

IL MIO & IL TUO
Sheet music, 1930
Bonfanti

1931
Calendar
G. Acquaviva

ALMANACCO ITALIANO
Almanac cover, 1934

**ESTATE MUSICALE
MILANESE**
Advertising fan, 1939

BERTELLI
Calendar, 1937
F. Romoli

GLOMERULI O GOCCE RUGGERI
Calendar, 1935
G. Guillermaz

BERTELLI
Calendar, 1932

BERTELLI
Calendar, 1936

COLLI FIORITI
Calendar, 1933
Alfredo Cavadini

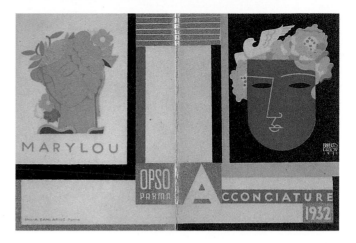

OPSO PARMA
Calendar, 1932
Erberto Carboni

BERTELLI
Calendar, 1939
F. Romoli

TENDENZE SPORTIVE
Calendar, 1935

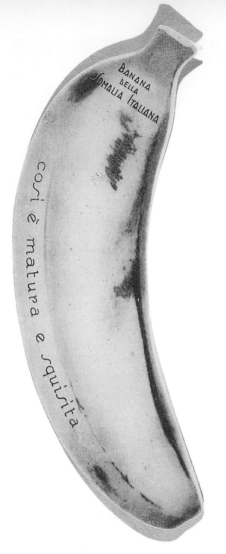

SEGNILIBRI
Bookmarks, 1930s

LA CITTÀ DI ABACO
Children's book (front and back cover), 1928
Antonio Rubino

L'ARCO DEI SETTE COLORI
Children's book (front and back cover), 1928
Antonio Rubino

Futurist fashion designers produced garments and textiles with outrageous graphics, such as Fortunato Depero's vest (page 122), but their influence on mass-market fashion was minor. Italy had a long tradition of shoe and headwear manufacturing, and some of the country's finest artists were employed to promote these products. Nevertheless, a graphic revolution in the field of fashion advertising occurred in the late twenties with a shift from what historian Giuseppe Priarone refers to as "idea-characters," the metaphoric mascots pioneered by Leonetto Cappiello, to the "idea-goal" devised by Sepo (neé Severo Pozzati, 1895-1983). The concept is here represented by Sepo's poster for Tortonese (page 123), a clothing manufacturer (originally called La Merveilleuse but forced to cha ge its name owing to a law prohibiting Italian busin ss from having foreign-sounding names). Sepo created a unique fashion symbol by overlapping a female figure with a mannequin, whose shape is formed by a ribbon. The poster reveals the confluence of Art Moderne styling and Cubist composition common to much Italian graphic design.

BIANCO
Department store
advertisement, 1926
Sepo

PARANASS

IL SOPRABITO IMPERMEABILE PER TUTTI I TEMPI

PARANASS
Raincoat label, 1931

BORRI
Shoe label, 1928

DEPOSITATA

MALÚ
Clothes label, 1938

PANICOTTO FUTURISTA
Vest, 1923-4
Fortunato Depero

CLAUDIO
Clothes label, 1941

IVOREA
Rayon label, 1933

QUINTÈ
Label for shoes, c. 1930

RIVELLA
Advertisement for furs, 1932
Erberto Carboni

125

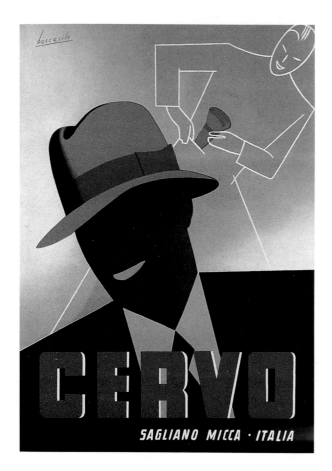

CERVO
Poster for rainhat, 1935
Gino Boccasile

BORSALINO
Poster for hats, c. 1938

Graphics for industry during the twenties and thirties were at once sophisticated and naive. Should technology be given a human face, or should the machine be glorified on its own terms? Within the Futurist ranks there was no question that the machine was sacred. But Futurism was not embraced by many Italian businesses. Company trademarks reveal a certain timidity — graphic puns and anthropomorphized or comic figures were used to individualize what critics called the depersonalization of mass production. The earliest industrial images were similar to those used to depict agriculture; industry was characterized as a muscular hero expending great energy to accomplish the task at hand. Eventually the machine and factory were celebrated for their own inherent virtues. And soon the robot — as used in Futurist advertising — became a comic, and therefore friendly, personification of industrial achievement. That Italy was unequivocally industrialized by the late twenties was demonstrated graphically by the increased number of manufacturing motifs used in everyday advertising and design.

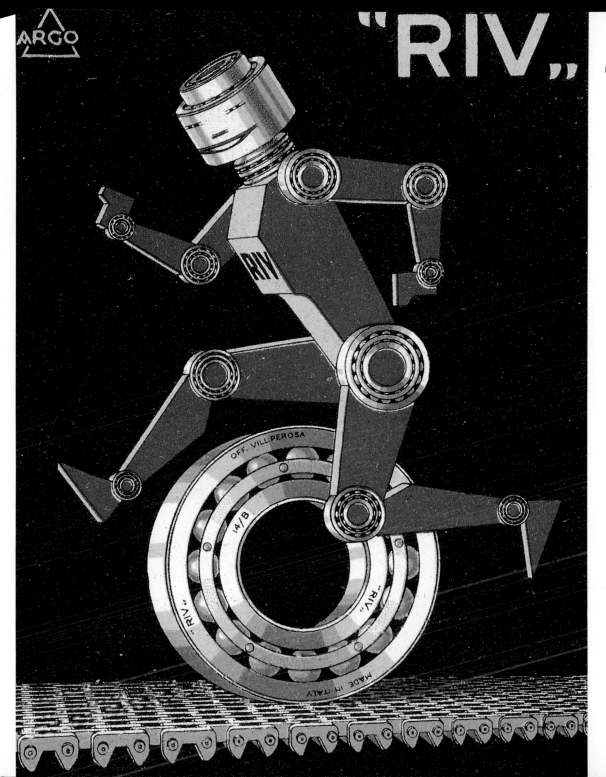

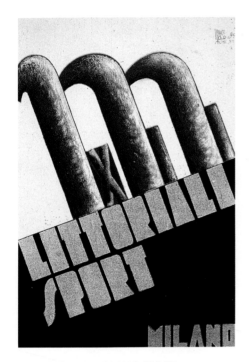

LITTORIALI SPORT
Postcard for sports fair, 1934
Latis

**4ᴬ FIERA INTERNAZIONALE
DEL LIBRO**
Poster stamp for book fair, 1931
Ninoz

XII FIERA DI PADOVA
Poster stamp for city fair 1930
Lucio Venna

CAMPIONATI MONDIALI DI CALCIO
Poster for soccer game, 1934
Mario Gros

MOSTRA INTERNAZIONALE
DELLE INDUSTRIE DEL CUOIO
Poster stamp for exhibition, 1931
Marcello Nizzoli

FIERA NAZIONALE
DELL' ARTIGIANATO
Postcard for fair, 1937
Giovanni Cappelli

ESTATE FRIULANA
Poster for festival, 1935
U. Grignaschi

VIᵃ MOSTRA MERCATO

VIᵃ **MOSTRA MERCATO**
Postcard for fair, 1936
Giuseppe Riccobaldi

133

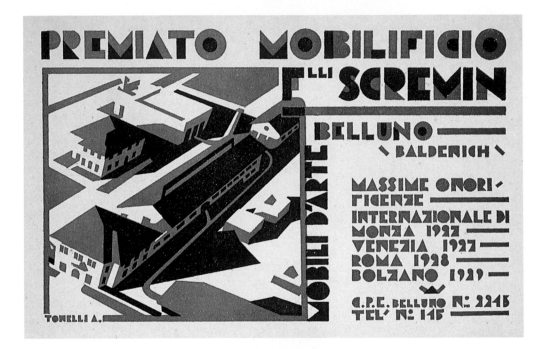

CANTÙ ALLA FIERA DI MILANO
Postcard for fair, 1934

LUBRIFICANTI FIAT
Advertisement for motor oil, 1930
Marcello Nizzoli

DA LEONARDO A MARCONI
Textbook cover, 1932

MOSTRA DELLA LUCE
Postcard for exhibition, 1933
Virgilio Retrosi

Making art reflect aspects of everyday life was not as revolutionary as the Futurists might have thought, for around the turn of the century many producers of sundries, cosmetics, and other quotidian products used modern conceits in their package designs. By the mid-twenties Art Moderne was applied to a variety of beauty and hygenic products, such as perfumes, talcs, bath oils, soaps, and toothpastes — even medicines. Though influenced by trends in modern art these stylish labels and packages, well suited to graphics that symbolize luxury and leisure, resulted primarily from competition on the shelves and racks of the *farmacias*. Store windows offered exuberent displays of Art Deco graphics. Cigarettes were also swathed in appealing imagery. Since Italians consumed them like candy, cigarettes were often packaged and promoted like confections, using motifs that suggested both adventure and chic. Delightful product graphics were applied to stationery and writing implements as well. Imaginatively designed pen-nib and pencil boxes brightened up the shelves and diverted the consumer's eye.

OVENALL
Poster for toothpaste, 1942
Zoltan Tamasi

CANTELE
Bath oil label, 1929

BERTONI
Package for toothpaste, 1933

KOLAPEPTIDE
Advertisement for tonic, 1937

TERGOL
Feminine hygiene product, 1929

FIORELLINI
Talc label, c. 1940

CIPRIA DORIA
Powder label, c. 1935

LINETTI
Perfume package, c. 1935

CARLO TACCHINI
Shaving cream label, 1928

S. A. ANTONIO
Tonic label, 1934

BEBÉ
Soap label, 1944

PETALIA
Powder package, 1928

OSSIGENAL
Bath oil label, 1937

143

CELLA
Shampoo label, 1934

BERTONI
Shampoo label, 1935

LILIA
Powder label, 1935

CIPRIA NOTTON
Powder package, 1935

NUOVO FIORE
Soap label, 1936

MERYBELL
Perfume label, 1936

OMEGA
Poster for watches, 1934
Mario Gros

OMEGA
Poster for watches, 1937
Guido Bonacini

PRESBITERO
Penpoint samples, c.1932
Franco Signorini

QUADRATINO DISEGNATORE
Notebook cover, 1934

DORIS
Pencil package, c. 1937

PRESBITERO
Pencil package, 1938

FILA
Pencil label, 1938

FILA
Pencil package, 1935
D. Tofani

At the turn of the century advertising posters were responsible for more than half the sales of Italian goods, especially liquor. Wine has always been one of Italy's flourishing industries — as early as 1900 Chianti was exported to virtually every "non-dry" country in the world — and liquor advertisements were the paradigms of publicity. "This explains the numerous beautiful posters," wrote N.G. Fuime in 1926, "which cover one-third of any Italian wall." No other distiller of spirits understood the value of a consistent graphic identity better than Campari, whose graphic designs were created by some of Italy's leading artists. Most extraordinary are the ads, posters, and publications designed in the thirties by Fortunato Depero, whose humorous, cubistic approach represents the most polished use of the Futurist style. Liquor companies were not alone in exploiting appetizing graphics; packages and promotions for Lazzaroni baked goods, Perugina candy, and Buitoni and Motta foods were created by Italy's most respected designers. In a country where meals are rituals, the graphics of food and drink were a feast for the eye.

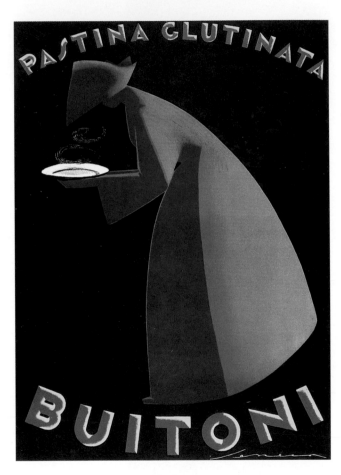

BUITONI
Poster for pastina, c.1932
Federico Seneca

BUITONI
Poster for pastina, c. 1934
Federico Seneca

ALA
Baking powder label, 1934

RIVALDO ROSSI
Wheat label, 1944

MORANDI
Rice label, 1944

ORZO IDROLITICO
Cereal label, 1940

STELLA D'ITALIA
Cheese label, 1924

CANARRI
Fruit label, 1938

CULTU FERTILIOR
Grain label, 1924

**MOTTA
PANETTONI**
Package, 1930

VILCO
Meat label, 1946

SIK
Cheese label, 1939

VIGANÒ
Pasta label, 1945

IMPERIALE
Biscuit label, 1932

155

DOMENICO BRISTOT
Coffee label, 1934

TORINO

CACAO DI ATTILIO LATTES
Cacao label, 1934

BOTTEGA DEL CAFFE
Coffe label, 1930

CAFFE MOKARABIA
Cup, c.1938

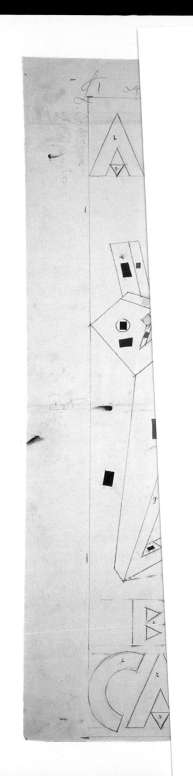

CAMPARI L'APERITIVO
Advertisement, c. 1930
Fortunato Depero

Italy is famous for its motor cars. Firms like Alfa Romeo, Lancia, Bugatti, and Fiat made the machines on which automotive legends were built. "The motor car industry, its affinities and accessories, has always been of great interest to Italians," wrote N.G. Fiumi in 1926 about the extraordinary number of posters produced at that time. In their reverence for speed the Futurists imbued the automobile with the power of a religious icon, devoting poems, paintings, and graphics to it. After liquor no other advertisements for industry were as ubiquitous, and no other manufacturer was as prolific with its advertising as Fiat. During the twenties Fiat was the largest automotive firm in Europe, and the first to open a special advertising department. Racing added to the allure of the automobile, and posters that idealized this test of man and machine were commonplace. The airplane was also a symbol of futuristic wonder. It is not surprising that Mussolini's own obsession with flying influenced graphics. These depictions were in turn used in ads for the travel and tourist industries, among Italy's most lucrative businesses.

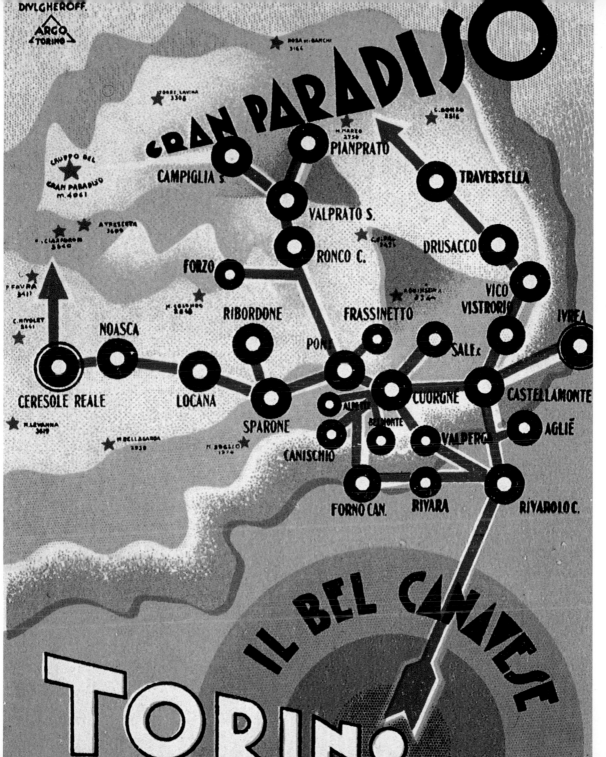

GRAN PARADISO
Travel poster, 1930
Nicolaj Diugheroff

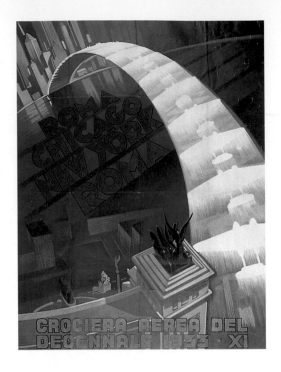

CROCIERA AEREA
DEL DECENNALE 1933
Poster for exposition, 1933
Luigi Martinati

CROCIERA AEREA
DEL DECENNALE 1933
Poster for exposition, 1933
Luigi Martinati

ALI D'ITALIA
Almanac cover, 1930
Bruno Munari

FIERA
Postcard, c. 1926

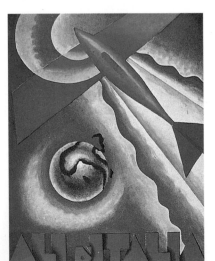

GIRO AEREO D'ITALIA
Magazine title panel, 1930

I PERIODICI
DELL'AVIAZIONE ITALIANA
Advertisement, 1935

CROCIERA AEREA DEL DECENNALE
1933
Poster stamp for exposition, 1933
Luigi Martinati

L'ALA ITALIANA
Bookcover, 1939
Yambo

CHAMPION
Poster for sparkplugs, 1928
Lanfranco Felin

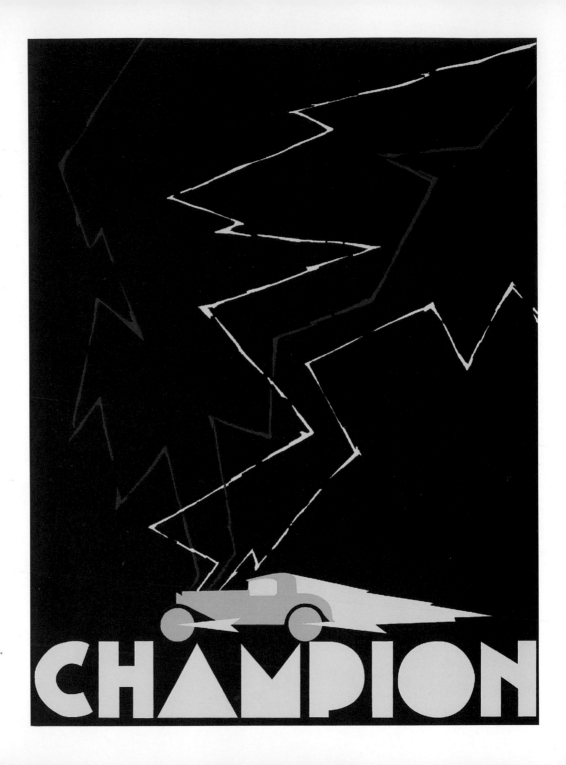

LAMPO
Poster, 1930
Marcello Nizzoli

MAG SPINTER SPARKPLUGS
Poster, 1929
Mario Sironi

SOCIETÀ ANOMINA PNEUMATICI
Logo, 1941

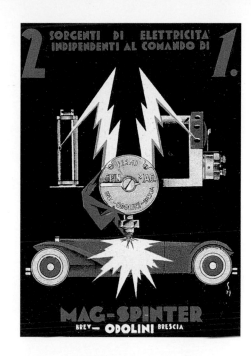

**VIII CAMPIONATO PROVINCIALE
AUTOMOBILISTICO**
Poster, 1930
Erberto Carboni

**IV CUNEO COLLE
DELLA MADDALENA**
Poster, 1930
Lucio Venna

AUTOSERVIZI LAZZI
Advertising fan, c. 1937

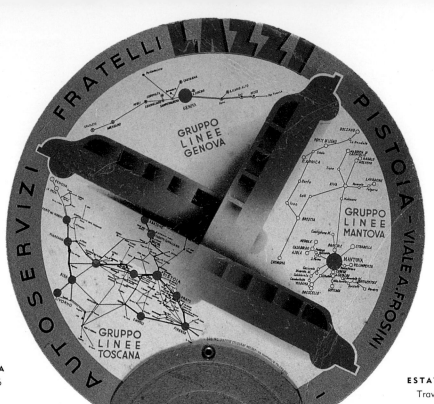

BIENNALE DI VENEZIA
Poster for exposition, 1936
Franco Signorini

ESTATE LIVORNESE
Travel poster, 1936

172

ITALIA
Magazine cover, 1938

BOLOGNA
Travel guide cover, 1932

ITALIA
Magazine cover, 1935

NAPLES
Travel guide cover, 1932

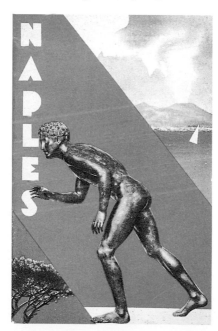

The Futurist rejection of the classical typographic canon disrupted "old snobbish aesthetic ideals." Their use of many discordant typefaces on the same page, an approach referred to as *Words in Freedom*, ignored entirely any semblance of symmetry. These raucous type designs were akin to comic book lettering, but the origin of the sharp-edged, block sans serif frequently used in Futurist book and magazine design is not clear. The artists who promoted it found hand-drawn letters to be well suited to the improvisational nature of their work — more expressive and freer than conventional types. Yet even when texts were set in preexisting type, the faces were often smashed, distorted, and otherwise deformed to emphasize the transient quality of Futurist poetry. Though typographic standards were routinely challenged, typography in Italy, the birthplace of modern type, was still a serious art. Futurism may have influenced many of the era's designers, but others, conforming to the spirit of Italianismo, continued to use nineteenth-century scripts and shadowed letters for contemporary logos.

VIAREGGIO
Hotel signs, 1930s

AVVISO

Durante le fermate a Saronno si ha il tempo sufficiente per acquistare, in stazione, una scatola dei famosi Amaretti di Saronno Lazzaroni

ACQUA RAPIDA

CARTE DA GIUOCO

INSUPERATE E INSUPERABILI

TUTTI I TIPI
REGIONALI
E TIPI ESTERI
COMUNI E DI LUSSO

STABILIMENTI
S.D. MODIANO
TRIESTE

TELEGRAMMA LAMPO VIA ITALCABLE

MILANO CONFEZIONI
Advertisement, 1935

AVVISO
Advertisement for Lazzaroni biscuits,
c. 1930

ACQUA RAPIDA
Label for shaving lotion, c. 1930

CARTE DA GIUOCO
Advertisement for cigarettes, 1930

LAMPO
Letterhead for telegram, 1929

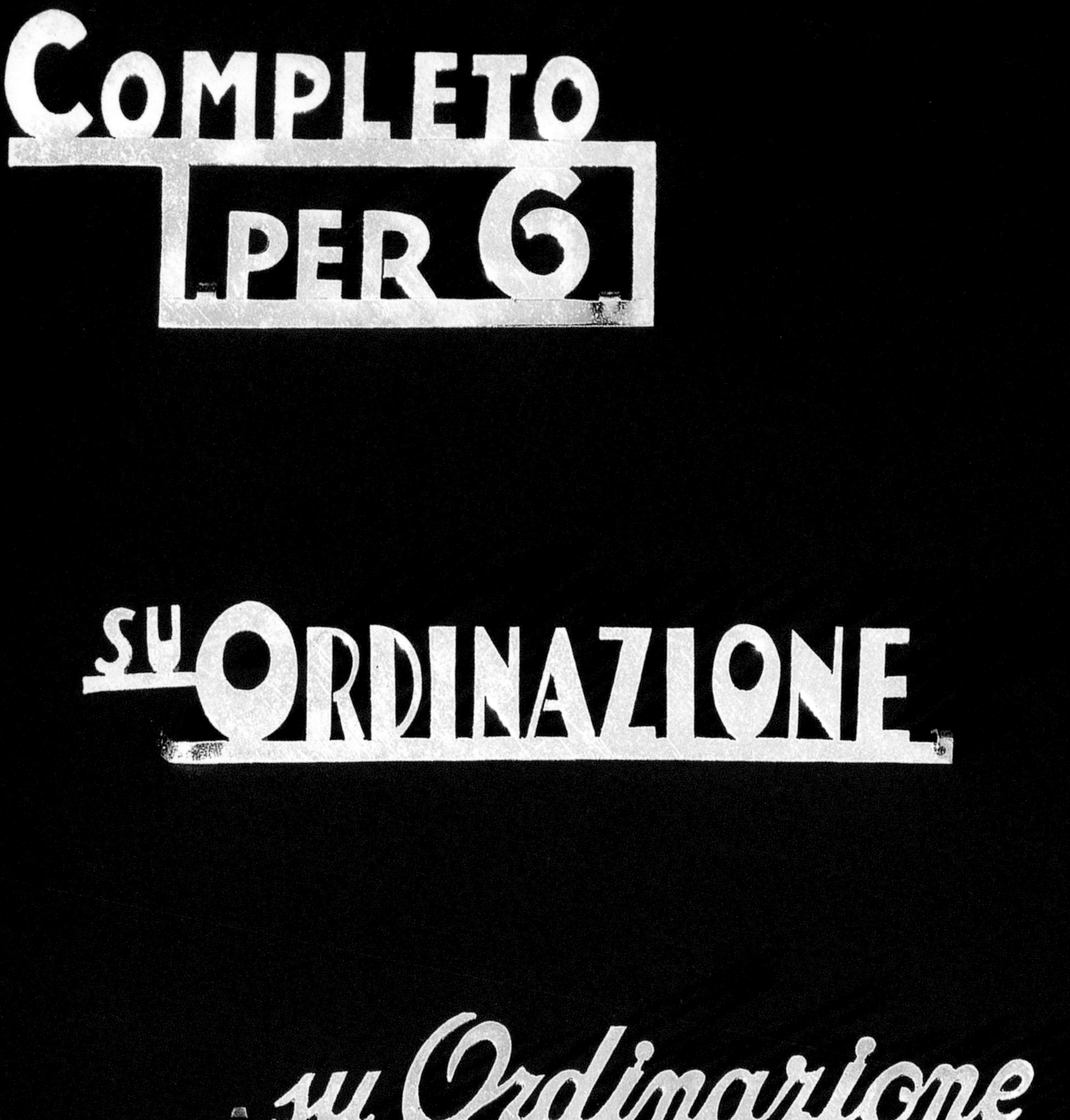

COMPLETO
PER 6

su ORDINAZIONE

su Ordinazione

Arrivi

dalle 13 alle 15

RECLAME

GER
MOD

England was the cradle of the Arts and Crafts movement. France was the birthplace of Art Nouveau. But Germany was the font of twentieth-century modern graphic design. German designers introduced simplicity and abstraction to *Gebrauchsgraphik* (commercial art), pioneered corporate identity, perfected *Marken* (trademarks), and founded design schools and movements that defined European design for the commercial age. German graphic design was a miscellany of intersecting ideas and styles influenced by the demands of industry and commerce. Under the rubric German Modern, numerous graphic styles comprised a national aesthetic.

Modernism, a slippery term century art and design and was covered the more mainstream Art in 1896 with the advent of *Jugend-* variation of French Art Nouveau, the constraints of academicism and When it was introduced through

that denotes progressive twentieth- ultimately the umbrella term that Deco style, took hold in Germany *stil* (youth style). A Teutonic *Jugendstil* was a reaction to both the excesses of ornamentalism. progressive art and design journals

such as *Jugend* (*Youth*) and *Simplicissimus*, as well as on the advertising posters then blossoming in the urban landscape, a new generation of artists expressed the zeitgeist through unprecedented graphics. This upstart "youth style" replaced stifling nineteenth-century Wilhelmian convention with color, geometry, and, most importantly, humor. Although *Jugendstil* was not quite as eccentric as its French and Belgian cousins—or as raucous as its Austrian sister, the Vienna Secession—it was a vibrantly illustrative and decorative style that altered the practice of applied art. Nevertheless, *Jugendstil* was but a bridge linking past and future.

Within ten years of its inception, *Jugendstil* was decried as bourgeois, and its decorative veener was gradually stripped off everything from furniture to graphics. In graphic design, a new method called *Sachplakat* (object poster) emerged that redefined the term *modern* and transformed *Werbekunst* (pictorial advertising) from ornate to minimal. Superfluous matter was eschewed in favor of aesthetic economy. All that was shown was a graphic image of the essential object (or concept) being advertised, and usually a line or two of bold lettering.

The first *Sachplakat* was designed in 1906, the invention of a young graphic artist named Lucian Bernhard. He was frustrated with the fussiness of his own work, and in one piece, a maquette he planned to enter into a poster competition sponsored by the Preister match company, he painted out all the *Jugendstil* elements he had reflexively added. After removing every nonessential component (a cigar, an ashtray, a checkered table cloth, and a few requisite *Jugendstil* nymphs), all that remained were two red matches with yellow tips set against a dark maroon background with the word *Preister* in block letters at the top. It was uncommonly spare, yet curiously eye-catching. One of the competition judges, an advertising agent named Ernst Growald, was not only immediately attracted by it, he declared that it was a work of genius. By awarding Bernhard first prize, Growald launched the career of a leading poster artist, gave life to a poster movement, and initiated a graphic style that dominated German advertising for the next decade.

Sachplakat was principally practiced by the Berliner Plakat, a group of kindred artists and designers represented by Growald's Berlin-based printing firm and advertising agency, Hollerbaum and Schmidt. Through posters that heroized the mundane, the consumer's attention was directed to unambiguous graphic images of commerce and industry—a typewriter, a pair of shoes, a spark plug, a lightbulb, an engine, matches. The rejection of artifice was consistent with German industry's desire to infiltrate the mass consciousness through

STILLER
Poster, 1908
Designer: Lucian Bernhard

increasingly more effective means. Artifice-laden posters along Berlin's wide boulevards were harder to read

from fast-moving cars and buses. The demands of the urban environment required simplicity.

Sachplakat prefigured the strategy currently known as branding, where a focus on mnemonic attributes

of a particular product or service is key to consumer recognition, but with the emphasis so placed, German

designers were required to make the objects that were to be promoted look even better than they were.

Fresh new tins, cartons, boxes, and bottles were designed by many of the *Sachplakat* artists, yet the poster

was still the most important selling tool. And *Das Plakat* (1910–21), Germany's most influential advertising

and poster journal (which had a respectable circulation abroad) promoted the virtues of *Sachplakat* and

celebrated its artists.

Edited by Hans Sachs, a Berlin dentist and president of the Friends of the Poster Society, *Das Plakat*

DIE WOCHE
Poster, c. 1908
Designer: Carlo Egler

attempted to wed business and art in a common cause. Its success was quantifiable. An overwhelming number of German retailers and manufacturers in the chemical, cigarette, and luxury foods industries employed posters and collateral print material to promote their respective wares. Similarly, the German Werkbund, an organization established to promote the production and sale of superior German goods internationally, propelled the applied arts—graphic design included—into the mass marketplace. From 1906 to 1914, posters advertising the bounty of these consumer goods spread the message faster and further than any other means.

Like *Jugendstil*, however, *Sachplakat* ultimately lost its novelty as repetition and mimicry reduced its commercial effectiveness over time. When *Sachplakat* no longer did its job, it gave way to what was more generally referred to as *Plakatstil* (poster style), an approach that offered a wider variety of images and methods. At this time a new graphic tool was also invented; a comic trade character embodying the attributes of companies and products that historian Virginia Smith calls "the funny little man." In her book *The Funny Little Man*, Smith explains that, around 1912, *Werbekunst* went in two directions. One approach was humorous and featured the stylized little character introduced by Valentin Zietara and members of the Munich Six advertising group. The other approach created the "gloriously perfect figure," a heroically realistic portrait of a man or woman found in posters by Ludwig Hohlewin, who later in the 1930s developed a poster image of the "quintessential Aryan."

Comic mascots bestowed personality traits on mundane, inanimate products that were more or less indistinguishable from the competition. They possessed mnemonic power—the ability to infiltrate the consumers' conscious and subconscious. The perfect figure, on the other hand, was the model of German perfection, a high ideal that the average consumer might rise to simply by buying and using the advertised product. The widespread use of these two approaches marked the dubious beginning of an era when theories of *Reklame* (advertising) were prevalent throughout the German advertising industry. The individual artist's intuition and talent, which had heretofore been the guiding factors behind most advertising, were quickly subsumed by psychological theories wed to the pseudoscience of propaganda.

By 1914, German advertising was highly sophisticated in Berlin, Munich, Stuttgart, and Leipzig, where an annual advertising exposition was held; but with the advent of World War I, everything came to an abrupt halt. Production of most nonessential consumer goods was significantly reduced, and *Gebrauchsgraphikers* (commercial artists) had little choice but to give their services to the nation. Wartime propaganda campaigns took precedence, and even oppositional satiric journals, notably *Simplicissimus*, became resolutely patriotic. Posters in the modern style were replaced both by a stylized realism that celebrated the state and by a grotesque fantasy that demonized the enemy. This was a critical period of German history and a time when progress in graphic arts might have been totally stifled, yet surprisingly a few dissenting artists produced antiwar messages in a progressive idiom. German Expressionism was the vehicle for the opposition.

Expressionism began in 1905 as an aggressively modern form of graphics inspired by traditional African art. Intended as a pure approach to artistic expression, it was started by a group of idealistic young artists called Die Brücke (the Bridge) who believed art was curative. A second group, Der Blaue Reiter (the Blue Rider), founded in 1912, took Expressionist art further into the political realm and fought against materialism while promoting spirituality.

Before the war, the Expressionists' call for social change was expressed in metaphysical terms. After Germany's devastating and costly defeat, many Expressionists rallied to the left. They produced print propaganda that defined the revolutionary spirit of postwar Germany's Weimar Republic, which was founded in 1919 after the abdication of Kaiser Wilhelm II. Although commerce and revolution do not usually mix, aspects of Expressionism's surface style were adapted in postwar advertising to promote cultural events and consumer goods.

As such, Expressionism turned into another casualty in the quest for novelty. It was not an entirely effective commercial style, although it was widely applied to advertisements and posters for some leading companies, including AEG.

Once in the mainstream, however, Expressionism became the object of derision, particularly by German Dadaists, members of the antiart art movement that rejected even the slightest hint of bourgeois artifice. Expressionism ultimately devolved into pure formalism to such an extent that by 1933, even Nazi propaganda minister Josef Goebbels favored making Expressionism Germany's national style.

Founded in Berlin in 1918, German Dada borrowed techniques from advertising to propagate its own cultural and political agendas. Dadaists promoted an anarchic typographic idiom as symbolic of the destruction of bourgeois values. Dada mirrored the crises within the Weimar Republic, which after World War I was struggling to bring democracy to a nation that had long lived under the iron fists of monarchs and the military. Through disruption of the status quo in art and design, Dadaists sought to change in culture what they were incapable of doing in the halls of government. They thus took to the streets with leaflets and newspapers that espoused Communist ideology and incorporated unconventional type and images to agitate among the masses. Whether Dada really had any effect on mainstream *Gebrauchsgraphik* is a subject for debate, but the movement did reflect a general rejection of antiquated design and had an influence on the New Typography, a modern method practiced by progressive designers who were taught at or influenced by the Bauhaus.

The Staatliches Bauhaus, founded in 1919 in Weimar, was a state-sponsored art and design school that, according to its founder Walter Gropius, was created "not to propagate any style, system, dogma, formula, or vogue, but simply to exert a revitalizing influence on design." The Bauhaus existed to prepare a generation of artists and artisans to deal with the demands of industrialization and its impact on society and culture, and Bauhaus typography and graphic design courses contributed to radical shifts in how *Reklame* was composed and styled. The Bauhaus's *Neue Typographie* (New Typography), startlingly austere for the time, was codified in 1925 by Jan Tschicold and characterized by a total lack of ornament, a rejection of drawn or painted illustrations in favor of photography, and a preference for asymmetrical layouts with gothic typefaces. Incorporating layout principles that emphasized clarity, dynamism, limited color (usually red and black), and photography—traits found in Dutch de Stijl and Russian Constructivism—New Typography epitomized modernity.

The Bauhaus attempted to establish a universal design language that the mass population could easily

NEBEL:
HORN BAHN
Poster, c. 1930
Designer: Keimel

understand, but not every German appreciated the cool neutrality of modern design. What might be called orthodox modernism lacked the humor—and the human touch—that characterized both the best and worst of German *Reklamen*. The majority of German commercial artists were not slaves to dogma, but followed (or created) popular fashion. The words "'modern' and 'old-fashioned' have no real place in the vocabulary of advertising art," wrote an advertising critic of the day. "They pre-suppose a standard which for the advertiser has naturally and rightly no meaning." Depending on the client's needs and the artist's penchant, however, certain attributes of the New Typography—such as asymmetrical composition and sans-serif typefaces—were routinely incorporated with traditional illustrative and lettering approaches, which produced a hybrid modern style.

German modernism was a synthesis of contemporary design approaches. In addition to the New

Typography and *Plakatstil*, German designers subscribed to the international trend for *art moderne* decorative typefaces; yet there was always more difference than similarity between Germany and the rest of Europe. German commercial artists appeared to use more humor and were less likely to mimic the fine arts than those in other countries. German Modern was more hard-edged than the design idioms of France or Italy, for example, which had a softer, streamlined sensibility. While these and other industrial countries resolutely followed the *art moderne* style (later known as Art Deco) out of pride or happenstance, Germany set its own course. In Germany, the term *art moderne* was replaced by *Gebrauchsgraphik* to denote the general practice of commercial art. The magazine *Gebrauchsgraphik* (1924–41), founded by F. K. Frenzel, was Germany's premier advertising and commercial art trade journal. It published in English and German and respectfully showcased the best of international graphic design. Leading French, Italian, American, and Spanish artists were given exposure, but German ingenuity, rather than international stylistic conformity, was always celebrated.

Germany produced some of the most imaginative and creative commercial art during the post–World War I era, and many of its leading designers, contracted to work for businesses abroad, had great influence on the world of advertising and corporate identity. After the Nazis' rise to power in 1933, however, when the Dessau Bauhaus was closed (the school had moved from its original home in Weimar in 1925), it was forbidden to use modern design or sans-serif typefaces such as Futura, which Goebbels called a "Jewish invention." Rigid, central-balanced composition returned and traditional (and often illegible) Fraktur type was touted as symbolic of the glories of the nation. While the Nazi party did produce a graphic identity system and visual propaganda campaigns that were unmatched in history, overall German *Gebrauchsgraphik* was reduced to cliché. By the outbreak of World War II, whatever remained of German Modern was dead.

The world's most advanced machinery was developed in Germany during the first decades of the twentieth century. Likewise, the finest industrial advertising was produced there, too. It is a testament to German artistry that such mundane objects as gears, rods, pistons, and pipes could be rendered with such beauty and humor. In "Advertising German Machinery" (*Commercial Art 1927*), critic Walter F. Shubert wrote, "The most difficult problem of all [is] how to make an attractive design out of machinery and work tools. . . . No wild fancies or freedom of conception will avail anything in this particular branch, however; machines and tools demand the most intimate knowledge of their production, full comprehension of their usefulness, and a technical insight into their capacity." Although some artists could render every truthful detail of a turbo, contrary to the warning against fancies, Lucian Bernhard's poster for Hommel, a company that makes precision tools, employs such wit and humor that the ordinary is immediately transformed into the extraordinary (page 207). Other industrial products—lightbulbs for example—were afforded fetishist attention. Capturing the verisimilitude of a bulb's delicate shape and crystalline appearance challenged most artists. At the same time, the need to differentiate brands from one another forced artists to find novel methods of achieving perfection. Every medium from woodcut to oil paint was used to create an eye-catching look. Color played an important role in German commercial art in general, and industrial advertisements benefited from bright hues and loud splashes. Of course, the funny little man was recruited when the object alone did not exert enough personality.

**KRONLEUCHTER-
FABRIK**
Poster, c. 1915
Designer: Julius Klinger

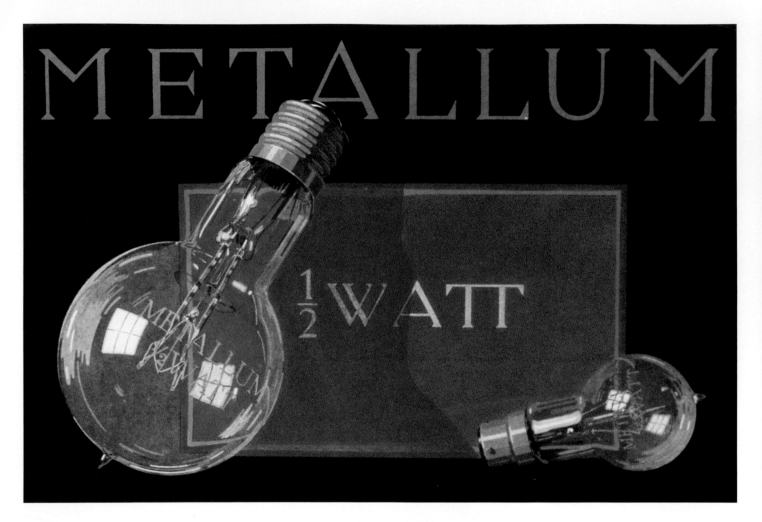

METALLUM
Poster, c. 1925
Designer: Willrab

CURRUS
Point-of-purchase
display, c. 1928
Designer unknown

LARME NICHT
Poster, 1926
Designer: Lucian
Bernhard/Fritz Rosen

TUNGSRAM
Package, c. 1923
Designer unknown

BLENDE NICHT
Poster, 1926
Designer: Lucian
Bernhard/Fritz Rosen

TORNAX
Poster, 1926
Designer: Willrab

**NAUCK &
HARTMANN**
Poster, c. 1912
Designer unknown

TON ZEMENT
Advertising
stamp, 1910
Designer unknown

**BEKLEIDUNGS
INDUSTRIE**
Advertising
stamp, 1925
Designer: Erik

HOMMEL
Poster, c. 1912
Designer: Lucian
Bernhard

GAS
Poster, 1924
Designer: Walter Dexel

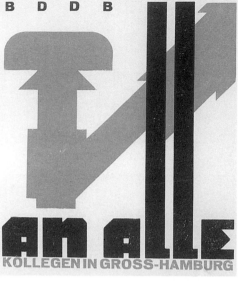

IM KAMPF
Advertisement,
1924
Designer unknown

GLAS
Advertisement, 1928
Designer: Karl
Schulpig

AN ALLE
Advertisement,
1924
Designer unknown

SZAKÁTS
Poster, c. 1920
Designer:
Otto Ottler

BOSCH ÖLER
Poster, c. 1914
Designer:
Lucian Bernhard

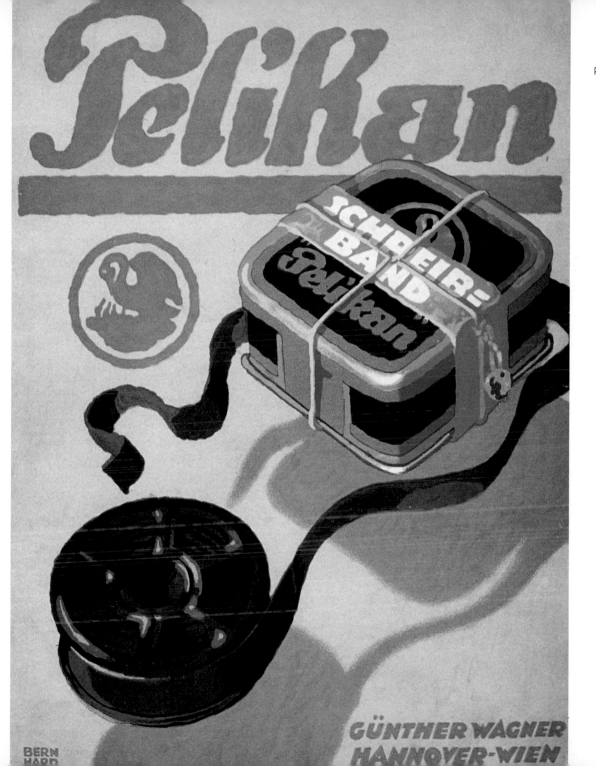

PELIKAN
Poster, 1920
Designer:
Lucian
Bernhard

MÜLLER
Advertisements, c. 1914
Designers unknown

PELIKAN
Advertising
stamp, c. 1930
Designer unknown

SCHIRMER
& MAHLAU
Advertisement,
c. 1925
Designer: Max
Bittrof

GRAZER MESSE
Advertising stamp,
1926
Designer unknown

BAFA
Advertising stamp,
c. 1930
Designer unknown

WALTER HELD
Advertising stamp,
c. 1910
Designer unknown

DÜSSELDORF
Poster, 1926
Designer:
L. Ten
Hompel

215

As capitals of commercial art, Berlin and Munich hotly competed with both Stuttgart and Leipzig, which were panting in second place. Berlin was home to Hollerbaum and Schmidt, Germany's foremost printer and the advertising agent for the Berliner Plakat. Munich produced Ludwig Hohlwein and "The Six," a highly successful confederation of Munich's other leading *Gebrauchsgraphikers*. While most commercial artists were generalists working for a variety of large and small companies and businesses, culture was the industry that pushed Berlin and Munich artists into the top of their profession. Huge quantities of advertising for film, theater, cabaret, and art exhibitions emanated from these two cities. Since many different talents were caught up in the cultural vortex, there was no single dominant style, although a fashion for *moderne* prevailed. In posters for films, for example, symbolism was applied for films in which establishing a sense of plot was more important than show-casing the actors; yet stylized realism was used when it was necessary to express the film's content literally. Photomontage, a modern graphic tool that was gaining adherents during the mid-1920s, was increasingly used and encouraged, particularly to advertise "noir" films with a modern sensibility. And photographs themselves replaced painted or illustrative art in design that incorporated the New Typography. Posters were the primary advertising medium, and pasting them on special kiosks was the primary means of dissemination. In addition, poster stamps—miniature versions of larger posters or original designs—were an important method of mass communication.

DIE TRUPPE
Poster, c. 1925
Designer unknown

OPIUM
Poster, c. 1925
Designer: Petau

MIKADO
Poster, c. 1928
Designer:
M. Schwarzer

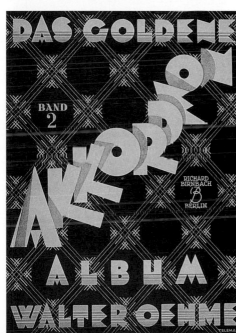

**1000
TAKTE TANZ**
Songbook cover,
c. 1930
Designer: Herzig

**DAS GOLDENE
AKKORDEON ALBUM**
Songbook cover,
c. 1930
Designer: Telemann

VOM 14. OKT. - 18. NOV. 1928. OFFEN 10-21ʰ

SCHAU
FENSTER
SCHAU

LEIPZIG.GRASSIMUSEUM.HOSPITALStR.3

WERBEKUNST
AUSSTELLUNG
Poster, 1925
Designer: Erik Murcken

GALERIE BANGER
Poster, 1926
Designer: Max Henze

ABGESCHNITTEN
Advertisement, c. 1928
Designer: Werner Epstein

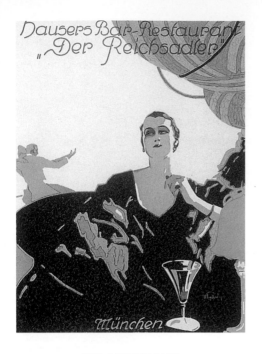

DER REICHSADLER
Poster, c. 1925
Designer: J. V. Engehard

MADAME DUBARRY
Poster, 1916
Designer: Mayer-Lukas

CHINA UND
ORIENT WAREN
Poster, c. 1912
Designer: Ludwig Hohlwein

GROSSE INTERN
AUSSTELLUNG
Advertising stamp, 1913
Designer unknown

NURNBERGER
KUNSTGENOSSENSCHAFT
Advertising stamp, c. 1923
Designer unknown

OSTMESSE
Advertising
stamp, 1937
Designer unknown

**DER GEDECKTE
TISCH**
Poster, c 1913
Designer: Julius
Gipkens

**AUSSTELLUNG
ALT-CHINA**
Poster, c. 1913
Designer: Julius
Gipkens

Speed was an icon of the modern age, and getting from here to there or there to here was the theme of German transportation advertising. It did not matter by what means this was achieved—cars, trucks, trains, or bicycles. Perpetual motion was promoted through the conceit of the blur. Modern life was typified by quick passage. With barely a few stylistic tweaks and perhaps only a couple of motion lines, the *Gebrauchsgraphiker* could impart the impression of speed. In the Hirschbold poster (opposite page) the forward thrust of the racing automobile and truck is accentuated by the leaning buildings rendered in an expressionistic manner.

Objects were key to transportation advertising. The simulated motion lines of tire treads, for example, were emphasized as symbolic of speed. Even renderings of inanimate objects were graphically highlighted and positioned at angles in such a way as to suggest forward thrust. But, not every car, truck, or bike was presented in a state of motion. Cars were sold both as instru-

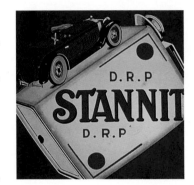

ments of speed and as objects of elegance, as the poster for DUX (page 228) reveals. Brand names were also emphasized. The poster for Opel (page 229) doesn't even show the vehicle, only a somewhat haunting portrait of a driver; yet even this otherwise static image evokes a sense of anticipation that the driver will soon take off for points unknown. The advertisements shown here are surprisingly sophisticated compared to others in this genre, which could also be very literal and uninspired. The most unusual is the Mercedes poster (page 230) designed in the manner of the Bauhaus in which abstract visual elements barely hint at the real object.

STANNIT
Enamel sign,
c. 1920
Designer
unknown

HIRSCHBOLD
Poster, c. 1925
Designer:
Johann B.
Maier

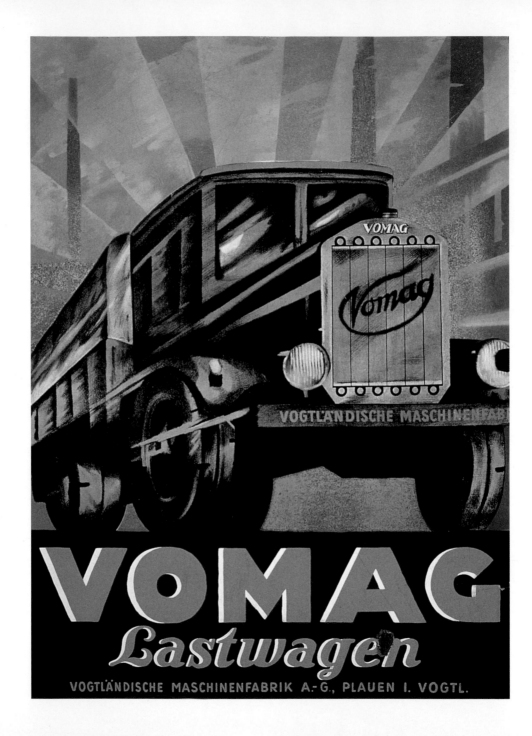

EXCELSIOR
Poster, c. 1922
Designer: T. Behrends

PETERS UNION
Poster, c. 1922
Designer:
F. Neumannsfred

NSU
Enamel sign, 1925
Designer unknown

OPEL
Poster, c. 1925
Designer unknown

DUX
Poster, c. 1913
Designer unknown

OPEL
Poster, c. 1914
Designer: H. R. Erdt

INTERNATIONALE
EINFUHR-MESSE
Poster, 1919
Designer: Ludwig
Hohlwein

ALLE FLÄCHEN
Poster, c. 1919
Designer: Lucian
Bernhard / Fritz Rosen

OPEL
Advertisement, 1927
Designer: Max Bittrof

"The new tempo of life has produced a vital change in the relations between buyers and sellers," wrote a critic in *Commercial Art 1927* about the nature of advertising displays found in shops throughout Germany. Demands on time no longer allowed the customer to browse the shelves for products leisurely. Advertising was needed to inform, but more importantly, to direct the consumer toward the target; products were no longer mere objects but destinations. Advertising cosmetics (the industry most promoted in Germany from 1925 to 1933 according to *Gebrauchsgraphik*), tooth-  pastes, bath soaps, detergents, and other household items required more than developing an identity; it demanded designing signposts to the very spot in the store where the product would be found. The job of the commercial artist was to invent a character or motif that pointed the way. The man in the clean white shirt and the woman in the fresh white dress for Persil detergent (page 235) not only attract the eye, but point the way. More than in any other Euro- pean advertising style, German *Werbekunst* set the standard for how the commonplace was monumentalized just enough to attract attention, but not so much that what was promoted discouraged the average consumer. Despite the hard sell of much German sundries advertising, humor was not entirely rejected, nor was elegance (depending on the purpose, of course). The advertisements for Syndetikon (page 238) are as witty as they are bold. The packages for Kramp & Comp body soaps (pages 236-237) are as visually enticing as they are functional. Even if the focus of German advertising was on the product *über alles*, fine artistry was the driving force.

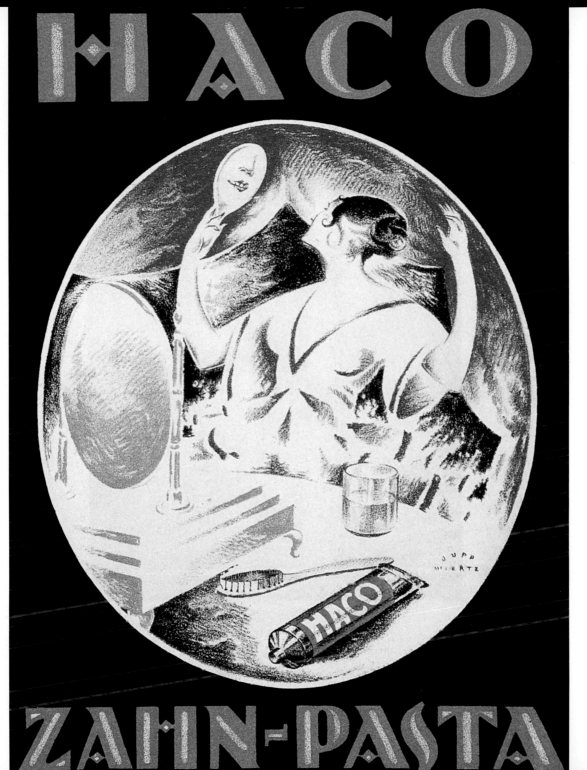

HACO

LUX
Enamel sign,
1925
Designer
unknown

**HACO
ZAHN-PASTA**
Poster, 1925
Designer:
Jupp Wiertz

HACO

JUPP
WIERTZ

ZAHN-PASTA

PERSIL
Enamel sign,
c. 1925
Designer: Joseph
Binder

Das neue Waschverfahren

Persil

Selbsttätiges
Waschmittel

PERSIL
Point-of-purchase
sign, c. 1928
Designer unknown

PERSIL
Enamel sign, 1929
Designer: Kurt
Heilingstaedt

KRAMP & COMP
Soap package,
c. 1913
Designer unknown

KRAMP & COMP
Soap package,
c. 1913
Designer unknown

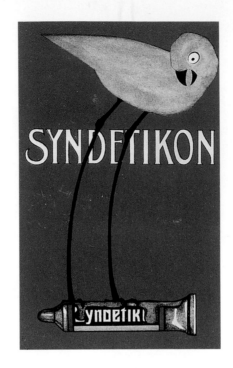

SYNDETIKON
Poster, c. 1914
Designer: F. H. Ehmcke

SYNDETIKON
Poster, c. 1914
Designer: Clara Ehmcke

RING'S
FLECK-ENTFERNER
Poster, c. 1914
Designer: Clara Ehmcke

239

After schnitzel and strudel, Germany is best known for beer and chocolate. As exports, the latter brought in a steady stream of profit around the World War I era. As domestic specialties, they were sought-after luxuries. The advertising and the packaging that promoted them were among the finest examples of an illustrative German commercial art. Confection shops were among the beneficiaries of beautifullly designed point-of-purchase displays, and the boxes and tins were adorned with vibrant colors and stylish designs. Gartmann (this page and page 244) and Stollwerck were among the leading manufacturers. Their ubiquitous packages, posters, and enamel signs synthesized Art Nouveau and *art moderne* styles into distinctive identities. These specimens were truly graphic confections. Beer was more conservatively promoted, but no less ubiquitous than the coffee, tea, and champagne (like Heinkel and Kupferberg Gold) advertising that filled the poster kiosks and shop windows in German cities, large and small. Many of the great German and Austrian poster artists contributed art and design to the wealth of advertising for food and drink, yet none was more prolific than Munich-based Ludwig Hohlwein (pages 241 and 242). *Hohlweinstil*, a stylized realism that made the commonplace romantic, eventually dominated German advertising. In 1906, a health food craze started in Germany, and Hohlwein was commissioned to create posters to promote "Alcohol Free Restaurants" and unprocessed foods. His skill at rendering made him the perfect choice for representing the natural bounty that zealots hoped would convince Germans to embrace nutritional purity over heavily advertised packaged foodstuffs.

FOOD & DRINK

MARCO-POLO-TEE

HACKERBRÄU
Poster, c. 1925
Designer: Otto Ottler

RIQUET PRALINEN
Poster, 1920
Designer: Ludwig
Hohlwein

KAFFEE HAG
Poster, 1910
Designer: Lucian
Bernhard

KUPFERBERG GOLD
Poster, 1913
Designer: Julius
Gipkens

KAFFEE HAG
Poster, 1910
Designer: Lucian
Bernhard

PFLAUMEN
Poster, c. 1913
Designer:
Carlo Egler

GARTMANN'S
CHOCOLADEN-
FABRIKATE
Enamel sign, c. 1910
Designer unknown

HEDRICH
Cookbook
jacket, c. 1913
Designer:
Carlo Egler

CURRI
Poster, c. 1922
Designer: "H/B"

MILCH
Poster, c. 1933
Designer:
Joseph Binder

Smoke wafted through German society with a vengeance and smoking had developed its own culture and rituals. In 1933, *Gebrauchsgraphik* reported that in the previous ten years, since the period of great inflation, more advertising money was spent by the German tobacco industry than by any other, except the cosmetic industry. Daily consumption of tobacco resulted in huge demand and obscene profits, which in turn made massive advertising campaigns both necessary and affordable. The cigarette (and to a lesser extent, the cigar) was the quintessence of formal simplicity—and even beauty. Many brands produced aesthetically pleasing oval-shaped cigarettes that were packed in stylish tins. While some of these packages were elegantly classical—adorned only with a coat of arms or other heraldic device—others were given a modern appearence. Manoli's colorful package, designed by Lucian Bernhard, was branded with a simple M in a circle that prefigured the bullseye brand later affixed to Lucky Strike. In

one of Bernhard's strongest *Sachplakat* images (page 250), a cigarette sits on the open Manoli box. Few other posters and advertisements come close to this for graphic eloquence or sales appeal. Other brands competed using a variety of visual tropes, including mascots (often well-dressed men or women, or exotic Turkish types). Identifiable logos were invaluable in promoting consumer awareness, and on occasion, humorous illustrations reinforced the serious hard sell. Fierce competition between brands with similar attributes allowed artists an opportunity to be imaginative. As long as the cigarette or cigar was represented in a flattering situation, emphasizing the fashionable nature of smoking, then the artist was given a long leash.

ENVER BEY
Point-of-purchase
display, c. 1926
Designer unknown

MOSLEM
Poster; 1914
Designer: Carlo Egler

PALM
Package, c. 1912
Designer: Carlo Egler

MANOLI
Poster, 1912
Designer: Lucian
Bernhard

GÜLEK
Package, 1921
Designer:
Herbert Bayer

MANESCO
Enamel sign, c. 1925
Designer unknown

GRATHWOHL-
ZIGARETTEN
Poster, 1919
Designer: Franz
Paul Glass

ADLER
Poster, c. 1999
Designer: Otto Ottler

"How can one describe those incredible times," wrote Stefan Lorant in "Sieg Heil," a history of Germany in the 1930s. "In the morning a newspaper cost 50,000 marks—in the evening, 100,000. The price of a single pair of shoelaces would have bought an entire shoestore with all its inventory a few weeks before. Beggars threw away 100,000-mark notes as they could buy nothing with them." Owing to Germany's immense war debt, the mark took such a dive that its value on the world market changed minute by minute. At the beginning of 1923, the American dollar was worth 7,424 marks. By August, the rate had risen to over a million; in November, the rate increased  to 600 billion; and by December, it skyrocketed to 4,210,500,000,000. The thirty-five Reichsbank print- ing presses, working night and day, could not print new denominations fast enough to satisfy demand or keep up with inflation, so a flood of *Notgeld*, or emergency scrip, was issued daily by towns and businesses. Since official Reichsbank notes were virtually worthless, most emergency money was worth even less, save for an investment of faith; yet since they were used as instru- ments of barter, *Notgeld* notes were redeemable for goods or services. With the permission of the government, local and private institutions could print bills cheaply, usually on newspa- per presses, on rag paper or cardboard. Since these printers were not standardized, the sizes, shapes, and designs were wildly inconsistent, and their images reflected the variety of talents and technology ranging from artful to primitive. Though many of the bills were beautifully ren- dered by professional artists and designers, others were scrawled by rank amateurs.

DER
UNIVERSITÄTS-
STADT JENA
Notgeld, 1921
Designer
unknown

KULTUR
U. SPORT
Notgeld, 1921
Designer
unknown

75 PFENNIG
Notgeld, 1921
Designer unknown

STADT-SPARKASSE
BIELEFELD
(front and back sides)
Notgeld, 1923
Designer: Herforder

OLDENBURGER
WOCHE
Notgeld, 1922
Designer unknown

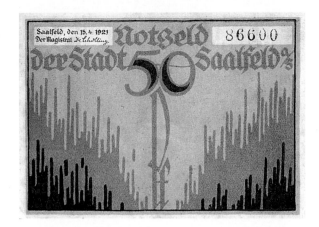

STADT SAALFELD
Notgeld, 1921
Designer unknown

GROSZENAU
Notgeld, 1921
Designer unknown

SCHÖPPENSTEDT
Notgeld, 1921
Designer: Günther
Clausen

259

50 PFENNIG
Notgeld, 1921
Designer: Rothschau

50 PFENNIG
Notgeld, 1921
Designer: Rothschau

25 PFENNIG
Notgeld, 1921
Designer unknown

50 PFENNIG
Notgeld, 1921
Designer: Nench

GEBR. PARCUS, MÜNCHEN.

50 PFENNIG
Notgeld, 1921
Designer unknown

OFFSETDRUCK GEBR. PARCUS MÜNCHEN.

ZWEI MARK
Notgeld, 1921
Designer: "P.M."

The Gothic typeface generally known as Fraktur is a spikey, medieval black letter that is as hard to read as it is ugly, but it was long held up as the German national typeface. Despite numerous attempts to aestheticize the basic form, progressive typographers believed that it was the essence of typographic tyranny. Early signs of revolution began with the advent in the late nineteenth century of *Judgenstil*-inspired typefaces, which replaced the sharp spikes with sinuous curves. When *Sachplakat* emerged, Fraktur was replaced by stark block lettering, often drawn by hand. While the spirit of this block lettering was Germanic, it was decidedly modern in appearance. It was also more eclectic, with swashes, ligatures, scripts, and other decorative tropes added on. Block lettering shared the stage with Expressionist-influenced woodcut rendered forms that were primitive and often unwieldy. By the 1920s, the demand in advertising for the *art moderne* sensibility in type forced the leading German foundries—Bauer, Flinsch, Stempel, and Berthold—to issue more formal, though no less quirky, alphabets adapted from letterforms designed by leading German poster artists. These type families were promoted through ostentatious specimen sheets to commercial artists throughout Germany. At the same time, a progressive typographic movement was emerging at the Bauhaus and under the banner of *Neue Typographie*, a new typographic method that favored assymetrical layout and sans-serif typefaces. Chief proselytizer Jan Tschicold's doctrine of asymmetry literally stood type on its side. The New Typography broke conventions and eliminated all ornament in favor of stark geometric forms—rectangles, circles, and squares.

P·WENDISCH

EIN SCHUTZ-ZEICHEN FÜR SIE!

ES BEDEUTET VOLLENDUNG FÜR DIE ERZEUGNISSE DER FIRMA...

F. GUHL & CO.

GRAPHISCHE KUNSTANSTALT UND KLISCHEEFABRIK FRANKFURT·M

VEGA-GESELLSCHAFT
Advertisement, 1920
Designer: Louis Oppenheim

HOCHBLOCK FÜR REKLAME
Type specimen, 1920
Designer: Louis Oppenheim

L. KRUSZYNSKI
Letterhead, 1923
Designer unknown

(opposite)
LUDWIG FLATAU
Letterheads, 1927
Designer: Paul Pfund

AUTORISIERTE OPEL-VERTRETUNG
GENERAL-VERTRETUNG ERNST MAG
FÜR BERLIN UND PROVINZ BRANDENBURG

LUDWIG FLATAU

AUTOMOBILE · MOTORRÄDER · WASSERFAHRZEUGE
REPARATURWERKSTATT · ZUBEHÖR ·
ERSATZTEILLAGER · TANKSTELLE

FERNSPR. WESTEND 2253
BERLIN -
CHARLOTTENBURG 5
KAISERDAMM 105

INTERNATIONALE MONATSHEFTE FÜR BAUKUNST · RAUMKUNST · WERKKUNST

DIE PYRAMIDE

SIEBEN STÄBE · VERLAGS-UND DRUCKEREI-GESELLSCHAFT M·B·H· BERLIN-ZEHLENDORF

FERNSPR.= ZEHLENDORF

NR. 3007 · POSTSCHECK·

KONTO = BERLIN 33607

BANK-KONTO · DARMSTÄDTER

U. NATIONALBANK, FILIALE

BERLIN-LICHTERFELDE-W.

KONRAD BEICHT
ARCHITEKT B·D·A

HOCHBAU UND INNENAUSSTATTUNG
BANK = DRESDNER BANK, FILIALE LIEGNITZ
POSTSCHECK-KONTO = BRESLAU NR. 35073
BÜRO UND WOHNUNG = FERNSPRECHER 3225
ATELIER = FERNSPRECHER 3225

SCHILLER
Letterhead, 1924
Designer:
Otto Hahn

**RICHARD
LOEWENBERG**
Letterhead, 1924
Designer unknown

ED. OSIM
Letterhead, 1924
Designer:
J. G. Schetter

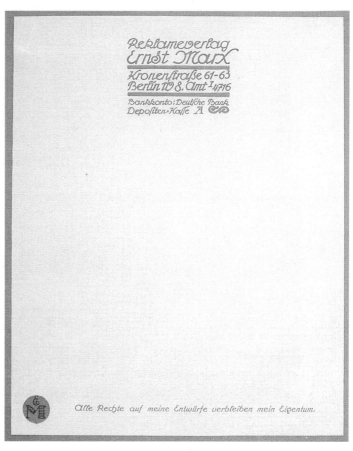

**HOHENZOLLERN
KUNSTGEWERBEHAUS**
Letterhead, c. 1913
Designer: F. H. Ehmcke

ERNST MARX
Letterhead, c. 1913
Designer: F. H. Ehmcke

RICH & RUHNAY
Letterhead, 1924
Designer: Heinz Weber

JOH. HARTLEIB
Letterhead, 1919
Designer unknown

STENCIL
Alphabet, c. 1928
Designer: Joseph
Albers

K. ZIMMERMANN
Letterhead, 1919
Designer unknown

KLISCHEE-FABRIK
JOH. HARTLEIB
BERLIN S 14
DRESDENERSTR. 34·35
TEL.: MORITZPLATZ 470

JOH. HARTLEIB
Letterhead, 1919
Designer unknown

abcdefghijklm
nopqrstuvwxyz
ABCDEFGHIJKL
MNOPQRSTUV

XYLO
Alphabet, c. 1927
Designer: Benjamin
Krebs

Import·Company
SUCCESSOR OF L. JEFFERSON SONS
26 TEMPLE PLACE BOSTON U.S.A.

IMPORT COMPANY
Letterhead, 1919
Designer unknown

DIE LO SCHRIFTEN
Type specimen, 1920
Designer: Louis Oppenheim

DIE BLOCK
SERIE IN DER AKZIDENZ
Type specimen, 1920
Designer: Louis Oppenheim

KINO
Advertising stamp, 1913
Designer unknown

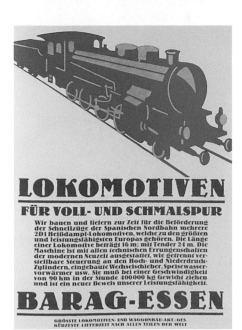

LOKOMOTIVEN
Type specimen,
1920
Designer: Louis
Oppenheim

PELZ
Type specimen,
1920
Designer: Louis
Oppenheim

SPORT TUT NOT
Type specimen,
1920
Designer: Louis
Oppenheim

A·M·A
Type specimen,
1920
Designer: Louis
Oppenheim

SPA
ART

NISH
DECO

introducción

Art Deco invaded Spain from France in the early 1920s and occupied the Catalonian city of Barcelona for almost two decades. Spanish artists learned the French graphic language, combined it with German, English, and Italian accents, and developed a decorative visual dialect that we call *Deco España*. Barcelona was the birthplace of Spanish Art Deco, but by the mid-1920s Madrid and Valencia also adopted Art Deco as the principal commercial graphic style.

Little differentiated the look of Deco España from the French model. Spanish illustrators and designers, many of whom developed distinctive personal approaches, borrowed elemental forms that were originally published in such foreign advertising trade magazines as *Arts et Metiers Graphiques* (France) and *Gebrauchsgrafik* (Germany). In fact, French printing firms and advertising agencies virtually colonized the Spanish commercial art market by selling stock advertisements and custom-made posters to Spanish companies. Catalonia, which had long depended on French culture, welcomed these exports by leading French artists such as A. M. Cassandre, Paul Colin, and Jean Carlu. By the late 1920s, Catalonian advertising, book, and magazine design was largely identical to the French style, but Italy eventually exerted influence when the Milan-based Maga Agency opened an affiliate in Madrid and sold the reproduction rights of their leading Italian poster artists, among them Marcello Nizzoli and Leonetto Cappiello. J. Walter Thompson also opened a branch in Madrid to handle its General Motors account and thus contributed an American dialect to the Deco España mix.

The term *Art Deco* was coined in the 1960s, a contraction of *Exposition des arts décoratifs et industriels modernes*, Paris's 1925 landmark festival of style. In the 1920s and 1930s, Art Moderne, as it was commonly known then, was the first pan-global design style, and it was replete with a vocabulary of interchangeable visual conceits. It was enthusiastically embraced by Europe, Asia, South America, and the United States — almost any industrial nation accessible by air or sea. As a decorative veneer, Deco was applied to architecture, furniture, fashion, appliances, and, of course, graphics. Art Deco began in France just prior to World War I, achieved real currency there in the early 1920s, and continued until World War II. It began as a stylistic reaction to Art Nouveau's floreated madness and ideological Modernism's purist mania. While Art Nouveau had become too eccentric in its linear hysteria, Purism went to the other extreme by rejecting ornament entirely. Deco was, therefore, a mediating force, an attempt to be modern while remaining true to bourgeois aesthetic preferences for pleasing decoration. In Europe after World War I, Art Deco was the symbol of both progress *and* decadence.

Art Nouveau's naturalistic motifs — serpentine tendrils and plant stems — gave way to Art Deco's geometric patterns and smoother, sleeker lines. While streamlined elegance was Deco's defining attribute in furniture and fashion, in graphics Deco offered a wider range of possibilities as various historical sources were blended into a unique melody of au courant mannerisms. Deco's initial, or neo-classical, phase during the 1920s was characterized by a synthesis of ancient forms, stylized quotations from Mayan, Egyptian, and Asian sources that were made to be contemporary. The latter, or modernistic, phase, which lasted throughout the 1930s, borrowed European avant-garde influences, notably from Cubism, Purism, and Orphism, that imbued the style with the rectilinear sensibility of *L'Esprit nouveau*.

Art Deco was marketplace modernity, not avant-gardism in the anti-canonical sense of Futurism, de Stijl, Constructivism, the Bauhaus, and Dada. Deco was cutting-edge design with dulled edges. It gave the appearance of progress—or newness—but was rooted in market-driven conventions that began in the late nineteenth century. Deco developed into a code based on mannerisms that appealed to the most superficial and visceral senses of the consumer, and on that level it was targeted at various social classes and age groups. Since Deco's signature elements were rather varied, it could be adapted as fashions changed and thus remained current longer than most temporal design trends. Had the austerity imposed by World War II not put an end to it, there is no telling how long the style would have continued to influence popular art throughout the world.

Different nations imbued Art Deco with their own indigenous characteristics, but they also shared the traits that defined it as an international style. Airbrush was the common medium, streamlined typefaces were vogue, and ziggurats, lightning bolts, sunrays, and other kinetic undulations were prevailing motifs. Human and animal figures were commonly flattened and reduced to silhouettes, or sculpturally modeled to give a heroic illusion. In addition to adopting the entire catalog of these modernistic conceits, Deco España was further informed by progressive German graphic design, which leaned more toward functionalism than adornment.

The Bauhaus masters of the 1920s scoffed at the very thought that geometric typefaces and asymmetrical layouts, which they proffered as a functional anti-style and were codified by Jan Tchichold in 1925 as *The New Typography*, would have such a huge impact on a decidedly decorative style. But in Spain the influence was incontrovertible. Futura, Paul Renner's geometric, sans serif "typeface of the future," was very popular in Barcelona, and the Neufville type foundry, one of Spain's largest, had tremendous success as the importer of this and other Modern fonts from the Bauer type foundry, one of Germany's leading manufacturers. In addition, Modernist designers from Germany, Poland, and Hungary introduced Bauhausian graphic design to Spanish commercial artists in Barcelona. Historian Enric Satué in his 1985 book, *El llibre dels anuncis: Anys d'aprenentatge (1931-1939)*, suggested that this was the period of "collective euphoria that characterized the Second Republic, the first chance to modernize the country since King Carlos III."

Long before the Republic was reconstituted for a second time in 1931, Spain's legendary avant-garde artists had emigrated to Paris. Pablo Picasso and Joan Miró developed revolutionary methods and ideas that would later surge back across the border as influences in both fine and applied arts. But prior to the Modern and Moderne invasions of Catalonia, commercial art took two routes: Modernisme and Noucentisme. Modernisme, which began around 1892, the year that the first "modernist parties" were organized by the painter Santiago Rusiñol, was an extension of the Art Nouveau and Secessionist movements in France, Belgium, Austria, and Eastern Europe, which were known for translating natural forms into ornate designs. In architecture, Antoni Gaudí was its champion, and the Church of La Sagrada Familia still stands as a monument to Modernisme's naturalism. In graphics, Ramon Casas and Alexandre de Riquer lead the way with posters that echoed the work of Czech-born Alfonse Mucha, who produced most of his posters in Paris but created some influential ones for Spanish businesses. Noucentisme, developed by Eugeni d'Ors in 1906, sought to regenerate culture through a philosophy that rejected late nineteenth-century Medievalism and esoteric Modernisme yet respected Spain's Classical and Mediterranean traditions. The Noucentisme view was rooted in a belief in the human capacity to create order, even against the unleashed forces of nature. Like Italy's historicist Novocento movement, Noucentisme's Mediterranean flavor was typified by idealized realism and didactic allegorization.

The transition from Noucentisme to Deco España occurred rapidly after World War I, yet the two styles continued to coexist and even influence each other. Deco completely overtook its challenger during the 1930s, when Spain made the leap from monarchy to republic and experienced the kind of social, cultural, and political upheavals that invite artistic revolution. The Republican Avant-Garde, as Satué called the movement from Historicism to Modernism, was a groundswell that introduced radical manifestations such as Cubism and Surrealism into Spanish art. Ultimately these forms were more or less absorbed into graphic design. Cubism, for example, entered typography in the form of decorative alphabets that were informed by Picasso's collages, and Surrealism's displaced realities and absurd narratives were applied to certain pictorial posters.

In the Republic, a move toward a freer economy offered new opportunities for manufacturers and merchants to expand their commercial horizons. Deco España quickly became the unofficial national style that linked the Spanish Republic to the rest of the industrialized world. Deco graphics were used inside Spain to promote many of the same products and services that signaled progress elsewhere and outside Spain to project its comparable standing with other leading mercantile nations. A Spanish mass market developed for appliances, furniture, fashions, and publications that were styled in contemporary idioms. Whereas design had played a subordinate role in the past, Patricia Molins and

Carlos Pérez (*Giralt Miracle and Typography*, 1996) believe that "In the twenties . . . 'graphic arts' as a craft gave way to that of 'graphic industries,' accompanied by the mechanization and specialization of printing establishments and the introduction of photography as an essential medium for reproduction." Initially, printers took sole responsibility for the conception and manufacture of advertisements and posters, but with the advent of industrialization and commercialization, designers became the predominant creators of visual form. Some of the leading printing concerns transformed themselves into advertising agencies that both represented artists and convinced Spain of the promise of design as a cultural force.

Catalonian businesses were very willing to spend money on good advertising design, and Barcelona became the hotbed of the graphic industry in Spain. One of its most influential printing and advertising establishments, Seix i Barral, recruited talented designers from the rest of Europe. In 1929 the firm hired a layout artist from the prestigious Studio Daeger in Paris, a German émigré whose name was Schuwer, whom Enric Satué identifies as an example of the elevation of anonymous commercial artist/printers into modern practitioners working exclusively and aesthetically with type and image. "He was the first one in Barcelona to work with the concept of graphic design, which was unseen at the time." This influx of foreigners, and the parallel development of native talent prompted what Satué called an "advertising revolution."

In Barcelona, as in other cities in Spain, advertising became a commercial necessity; and what began as an anonymous profession rooted in mundane nineteenth-century typographic convention became a wellspring of unprecedented graphic experimentation. Successful advertising agencies introduced popular designers to a public that appeared to enjoy the new visual stimuli. When the Barcelona-based Myrurgia firm showcased the work of Eduard Jener and the Madrid-based Gal firm did likewise for Federico Ribas, they invested the Deco vocabulary with a distinctly Spanish idiom.

"This period," Satué writes, "surprises us for the amazing capacity for the masses to accept and consume products advertised, labeled, or lettered with avant-garde graphics." An increase in new and repackaged wares also gave rise to graphic experimentation. The products that benefited most from new advertising and packaging techniques included cosmetics, soap, food, drink, and tobacco. Gastronomy was the rage in Spain's major cities, and a plethora of foreign cooking courses sprang up throughout the country, which in turn increased need for advertisements and posters for packaged food, restaurants, kitchenware, and even culinary magazines (including the smartly illustrated *Ménage,* devoted to the culture of cuisine). Art Deco graphics were also influenced by cinema, and one of the leaders of this genre, Antoni Clavé, influenced other advertising genres with his unique movie poster style that was half figurative and half Cubist. Catalonian impresarios enthusiastically embraced this type of advertising as the key to their success in the marketplace.

Prosperity, like the Republic itself, however, was relatively short lived. In 1930 the dictatorship of General Primo de Rivera fell. The following year, monarchist candidates were trounced in elections, King Alfonso went into exile, and the provisional government of the Republic was installed in Madrid. Two years later an ideological split within the Left enabled the nationalists to regain power, but in 1936 the Popular Front, a renewed alliance between democrats and left-wing republicans, won the elections with a little over half the popular vote. In the ensuing months, chasms grew between the extreme sides of the republican coalition, ending in violent discord between the various left-wing organizations. To preserve order and illicitly regain control of the government, the Right launched a violent counterrevolution that turned into three years of bloody civil strife. In 1933, General Primo de Rivera's son, José Antonio, had founded the quasi-fascist Falange, and by 1936 its militia was the sworn enemy of the Republic. In addition to the loyal regular army troops, the republican side was comprised of a loose alliance of democrats, socialists, anarchists, and communists. The rebels constituted an axis of nationalists, monarchists, militarists, and fascists. The war was viewed as a prelude to the Nazi and Fascist coups that followed elsewhere in Europe.

The Spanish Civil War was a war of bullets and posters. Graphic campaigns were waged by both the loyalists and the Falange, and Deco España was a tool for both sides, although it was primarily used by the Left. Emerging from the alphabet soup of left-wing political parties and labor unions — Unified Socialist Party (PSU), General Workers Union (UGT), International Anarchist Federation (FAI), National Workers Confederation (CNT), and Worker Party of Marxist Unification (POUM) — as well as from various government ministries, hundreds of posters were designed. They disseminated a variety of patriotic republican messages, from calls for enlistment to hygiene awareness. Carles Fontseré, a member in 1936 of the Syndicate of Professional Artists (SDP) (quoted in John Tisa, ed., *The Palette and the Flame,* 1979) said, "The popular and ideological character of the civil war turned the poster into an offensive and mortal weapon, [a] propagator of on-the-spot collective slogans improvised by the parties, syndicates, institutions of government and artists' groups."

Deco España was used by the Left, but the Right usurped the heroic leitmotif common in these political posters to romanticize their cause. Deco projected a progressive attitude rooted in tradition. The symbolism could be claimed equally by good and bad, right and wrong, and Left and Right. As the style of the era it was familiar to all; but given the commercial purposes for which it had been used, it was often too familiar. Critics of the style like Josep Renau, the director of Graphic Propaganda of the General Commissariat of the Republic, worried that the best artists working in this genre were not making effective propaganda, but rather fake fair posters, more like fine arts exhibitions and perfume ads. As exquisite as some of the republican political posters appear out of context, one commentator argued at the time that war is not an automobile brand, and selling it as such was ultimately wrong. Renau is quoted by Satué as having said, "We are fighting a war not selling a world's fair."

Despite the superiority of its posters, the republicans ultimately lost the shooting war. On April 1, 1939, the forces of Generalísimo Franco claimed victory and the war came to an end. Commercial advertising and publishing had come to halt during the Civil War, and by the end there was little left to advertise. Many of the leading stylists had fled into exile abroad or were relegated to internal exile under the unforgiving Fascist regime; those that stayed turned to other styles. Under Franco's rule, Deco España simply disappeared.

política

In 1936, during the first days of the Spanish Civil War, an explosion of posters erupted on the streets of Barcelona, Madrid, and Valencia calling on the loyal public to mobilize against Fascist rebel forces. In lieu of other mass media, these posters became the republican government's most effective and speediest means of communication. "Today the walls don't just have ears, they have learned to think, to shout," wrote George Orwell in *Homage to Catalonia*. Deco España was not the only style, but it was the one most commonly used for both propagandistic and cautionary messages. The many republican poster-issuing groups—government agencies, political parties, trade unions, youth organizations, international brigades, and the Council for the Defense of Madrid—expressed an acute sense of emergency that continues to give these sixty-year-old missives currency. Artists were required to wed aesthetics to concrete action. According to critic Luigi Longo, many of these posters, created by members of the SPBA, the Spanish artists' union, "succeeded in fusing the most vigorous experiments of contemporary art (from German Expressionism to Soviet Constructivism) with the simplicity and directness that are the tradition of the revolutionary message." (Quoted in John Tisa, ed., *The Palette and the Flame*, 1979.) The imagery heroized soldiers, monumentalized workers, and demonized rebels. Republican posters were aimed not only at city dwellers, but at illiterate *campesinos* (farmers). Slogans were key elements, and the posters employed familiar visual cues that urgently demanded the need for vigilance and patriotism. Alas, the republicans won the propaganda battles, but lost the shooting war.

1º GANAR
LA GUERRA
POSTER, 1937
ARTIST: PARRILLA

AYUDAD A MADRID

POSTER, 1938

ARTIST: CABAÑA AND
CONTRERAS

U·G·T·
P·S·U·

POSTER, 1936

ARTIST: L. LLEÓ

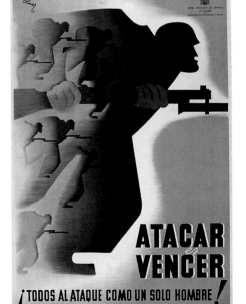

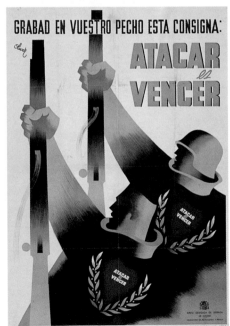

ATACAR ES VENCER

POSTER, C. 1937

ARTIST: A. OLIVER

ATACAR ES VENCER

POSTER, 1937

ARTIST: A. OLIVER

UNE A TU VOLUNTAD
LA DISCIPLINA
POSTER, 1936
ARTIST: ALEX HINSBERGER

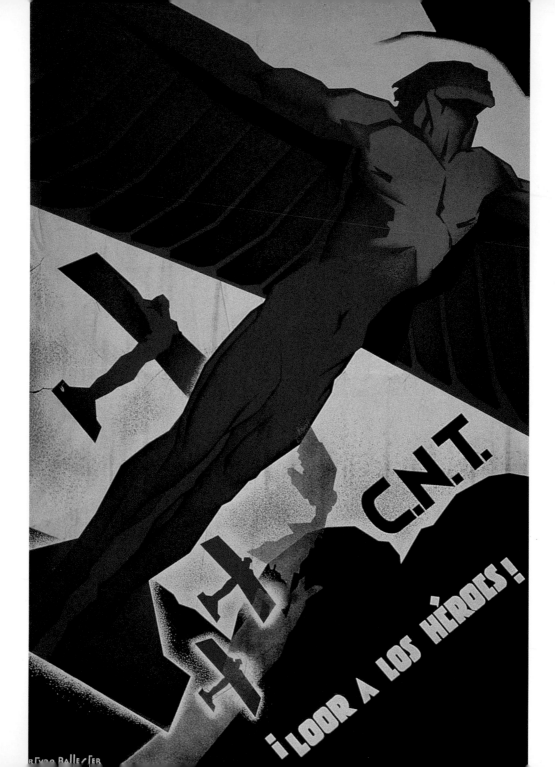

C.N.T.

¡LOOR A LOS HÉROES!

¡SALUD, HEROICO
COMBATIENTE DE
LA LIBERTAD!

POSTER, C. 1937

ARTIST: ARTURO BALLESTER

19 JULIO 1936

POSTER, C. 1938

ARTIST: UNKNOWN

SOLIDARIDAD
INTERNACIONAL
ANTIFASCISTA

POSTER STAMP, C. 1937

ARTIST: UNKNOWN

HAY QUE DAR EL
GOLPE DEFINITIVO

POSTER, 1936

ARTIST: SANZ MIRATTES

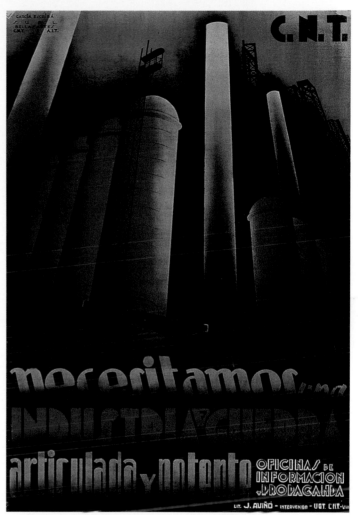

HACIA LA UNIDAD DE ACCIÓN
DE LA CLASE OBRERA
POSTER, 1937
ARTIST: GALLO

NECESITAMOS UNA
INDUSTRIA DE GUERRA
POSTER, C. 1937
ARTIST: GARCÍA ESCRIBA

MAS ESFUERZO
PRODUCCION
POSTER, 1938
ARTIST: RUEDA

ESPANYA EN GUERRA
POSTER, C. 1938
ARTIST UNKNOWN

ACCIÓN POPULAR
POSTER, 1933
ARTIST: X. ACEBO

ACCIÓN POPULAR
POSTER, 1936
ARTIST: AMBRÓS

cultura

Catalonia was the heart of Spanish avant garde culture prior to the Civil War, and Barcelona was the center for book and magazine publishing and excelled in drama, music, and sports. Advertising for these events was as respected as the arts they were promoting. "The commercial ad produces in us an emotion of infinitely superior order, [more] than the kilometers of qualitative painting that hang in our galleries," wrote Salvador Dali in 1928. The magazine *D'Acî i d'Alla,* which had been a noucentist publication, was among the many new masterpieces of design that appeared in the museum of the street—the newsstands and poster hoardings. Fully transformed from a historicist layout into a model of Modernist composition, this art and culture magazine balanced French Art Deco and German rationalism. Its covers were often decorative vignettes rendered in a Moderne style, and its interior was a veritable catalog of Modern concepts, including fine studio photography and photomontage as well as Modern fixtures such as sans serif typefaces, generous margins, and full bleeds. The new *D'Acî i d'Alla* also marked the first time an art director's name, Josep Sala, appeared on a magazine. Sala, a Catalonian designer, introduced Modern principles to periodicals and posters, yet despite his influence, a number of the most popular cultural magazines were more Moderne than Modern. *Nuevo mundo* and *Blanco y negro,* with their stunning Deco-inspired covers (but conventional interiors), drew their influence, like many book covers of the period, from the Spanish poster renaissance of the 1920s. Those posters, created for fairs, festivals, and performances, promoted modernity to the masses.

KINODEION
POSTER, C. 1932
ARTIST: BON

EL HOMBRE Y
EL MONSTRUO
FILM POSTER,
1934
ARTIST: ANTONI
CLAVÉ

BOLICHE
FILM POSTER,
1934
ARTIST: ANTONI
CLAVÉ

¿Y AHORA QUE?
FILM POSTER,
1934
ARTIST: ANTONI
CLAVÉ

EL HOMBRE
INVISIBLE
FILM POSTER,
1934
ARTIST: ANTONI
CLAVÉ

297

LA FARSA

BOOK COVER, C. 1931

ARTIST: ALONSO

LA FARSA

BOOK COVER, 1930

ARTIST: ALONSO

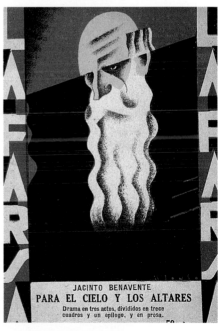

LA FARSA

BOOK COVER, 1929

ARTIST: ALONSO

LA FARSA

BOOK COVER, 1929

ARTIST: ALONSO

LIBROS
ANARQUISTAS
Y SERÁS
UN HOMBRE
POSTER, 1933
ARTIST: CIRRCIONE

DIA DEL LIBRO

DIA DEL LIBRO
POSTER, 1921
ARTIST:
J. MORELL

CÁMARA OFICIAL DEL LIBRO
BARCELONA

23 ABRIL

morell

NUEVO MUNDO

MAGAZINE COVERS

(CENTER)

1923

ARTIST: BON

(TOP LEFT)

1926

ARTIST: TONO

(CENTER BOTTOM)

C. 1926

ARTIST UNKNOWN

(CENTER LEFT)

1924

ARTIST: ALONSO

(TOP RIGHT)

1925

ARTIST: TONO

(BOTTOM LEFT)

1926

ARTIST: MANCHON

(CENTER RIGHT)

1924

ARTIST: BON

(CENTER TOP)

1920

ARTIST UNKNOWN

(BOTTOM RIGHT)

1925

ARTIST: TONO

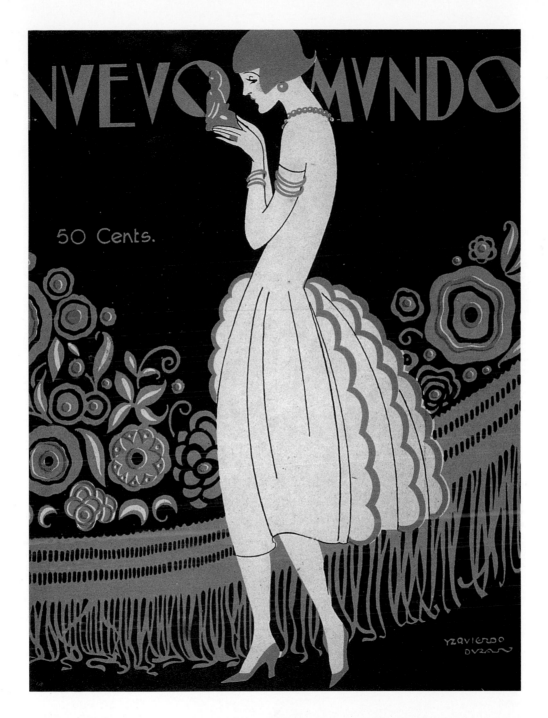

NUEVO MUNDO
MAGAZINE COVER,
1925
ARTIST: YZQUIERDO
DURAN

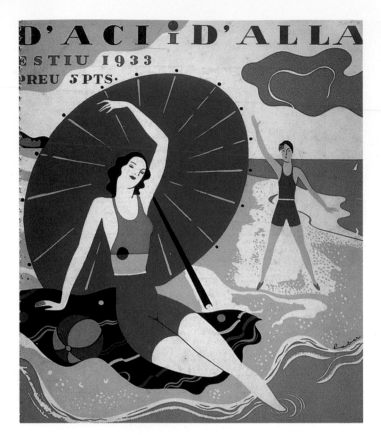

D'ACI I D'ALLA

MAGAZINE COVER, 1933

ARTIST: WILL FABER

D'ACI I D'ALLA

MAGAZINE COVER, 1933

ARTIST: WILL FABER

(OPPOSITE)

D'ACI I D'ALLA

MAGAZINE COVER, 1933

ARTIST: WILL FABER

REFLEJOS

MAGAZINE COVER, 1929

ARTIST: CORONADO

BLANCO Y NEGRO

MAGAZINE COVER, 1931

ARTIST: MASBERGER

BLANCO Y NEGRO

MAGAZINE COVER, 1931

ARTIST: ALONSO

industria

In Spain, the development of posters, calendars, postcards, and all other creative promotions became the job of what one critic somewhat hyperbolically referred to as the "Psycho Technician in Advertising." This was the age when advertising was first influenced by surveys and polls, and design was influenced by fatuous marketing data. This new pseudo-scientific field was purportedly based on an intimate knowledge of human psychology—the possibilities of propaganda to influence man's thought and action—wed to contemporary media techniques that could be applied to different needs. Despite an attempt to make graphic design into a more rational field, graphic artists were not scientists, intuition played a larger a role than ever, and style ultimately prevailed over any scientific attempt to target the perfect message to the right consumer. In some cases, companies doing business internationally, such as Philco and Ford, simply imported their own visual identities (or dictated them to Spanish artists) from their countries of origin. Other companies adapted their messages to what they believed the Spanish public wanted to see. Art Deco was applied to industrial products like automobiles that signaled progress, as well as to those like boilers, that needed a symbolic kind of recognition in the marketplace. The challenge for the commercial artist was how to give industrial wares a veneer that made them mythic and beautiful. Many of the predictable graphic motifs used to signify industry—smokestacks, factories, and heroic figures of workers—were drawn from a lexicon of universal symbols, but tweaked with a Spanish accent.

1ª **SETMANA**
COTONERA
POSTER, 1931
ARTIST:
L. MUNTANÉ

RADIO
BARCELONA
MAGAZINE
COVER, 1933
ARTIST: AVANTO

RADIO BARCELONA

Barcelona, 23 Septiembre 1933

40 cts.

PHILCO

POSTER, C. 1928

ARTIST: J. MORELL

CATALUNYA RADIO

MAGAZINE COVER, 1934

ARTIST: SERGI CORTÉS

CATALUNYA RADIO

MAGAZINE COVER, 1934

ARTIST: MARTÍNEZ SURROCA

RADIO ASSOCIATÓ

DE CATALUNYA

TRADEMARK, C. 1929

DESIGNER UNKNOWN

ACUMULADORES DININ
ADVERTISEMENT FOR BATTERY,
1929
ARTIST UNKNOWN

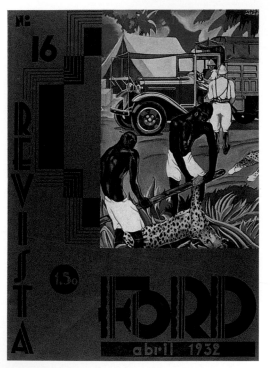

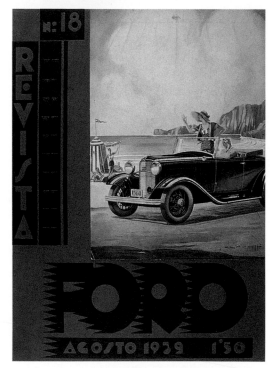

REVISTA FORD
MAGAZINE COVER, 1932
ARTIST: SAINZ DE MORALES

REVISTA FORD
MAGAZINE COVER, 1932
ARTIST: CERVELLÓ

eba

AUTOMÓVILES

**EL COCHE
DE LA ÉLITE**

¡Primero en su primer año! Elba se siente obligado a expresar públicamente su agradecimietno a usted y a las numerosísimas personas que, al adquirir un Elba, han demostrado su confianza en las afirmaciones de Elba, y le han permitido realizar tan destacado "record".

Es opinión generalizada que tal popularidad debe de ser merecida. Es cierto. Pero, para ganarla, incluso un coche tan acabado como Elba, necesita un público, un público inteligente, libre de los prejuicios que imponen las costumbres, un público capaz de justipreciar la revolución hecha por Elba en las reglas, al parecer inamovibles, que en los coches ligeros regían a la comodidad y al rendimiento.

El sentido crítico de este público, y las normas de prudencia que en 1930 presidieron a las compras, avaloran los fundamentos de cada una de las ventajas que Elba ofrece. De ahí que el número de compradores fuera creciendo.

El resultado es una página de oro en la historia del automóvil. Elba en su primer año ganó el primer puesto, adelantándose en más de 25 % al que ocupa el segundo lugar. Esta cifra es de por sí elocuente. Elba el ganador, da a usted sus más expresivas gracias.

Sólo Elba, que dispone de los enormes recursos y facilidades de Americán S. A. E., puede ofrecer en sus coches todas las ventajas que merecen sus propietarios.

El éxito de Elba no es accidental, es la resultante natural de un producto esmeradamente diseñado, estupendamente construído y vendido al precio más bajo posible... El primer puesto en las ventas significa un máximo valor que sólo Elba puede brindar.

INDREU
LETTERHEAD, 1933
DESIGNER UNKNOWN

FERRETERIA RAFOLS S.A.
LETTERHEAD, 1933
DESIGNER UNKNOWN

SOCIEDAD ANONIMA
MARIANO VILA
LETTERHEAD, 1933
DESIGNER UNKNOWN

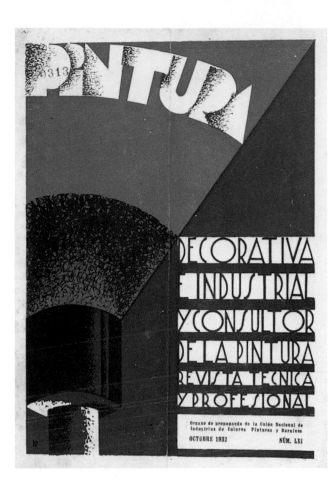

PINTURA

MAGAZINE COVER, 1932

ARTIST: F.F.

FILLAT

LOGO FOR MANUFACTURER,

C. 1928

DESIGNER UNKNOWN

NAGSA

CATALOG COVER, C. 1929

ARTIST UNKNOWN

I.B.Y.S.
LOGO FOR MANUFACTURER,
C. 1929
DESIGNER UNKNOWN

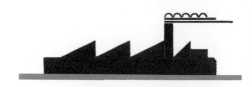

CONSTRUCCIONES
LOGO FOR MANUFACTURER,
C. 1930
DESIGNER UNKNOWN

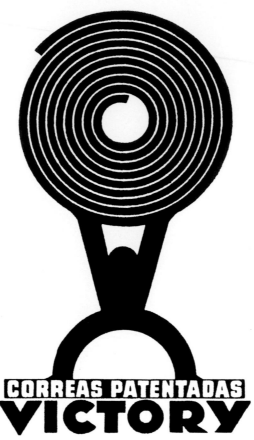

**MANUFACTURAS
IMA, BARCELONA**
LOGO FOR MANUFACTURER,
C. 1930
DESIGNER UNKNOWN

ROLON
LOGO FOR PUBLISHER,
C. 1928
DESIGNER UNKNOWN

VICTORY
LOGO FOR A TEXTILE FIRM,
C. 1930
DESIGNER UNKNOWN

AUXILIO DE INVIERNO
POSTAGE STAMP, C. 1934
ARTIST: K. CERNY

CAJAS DE CARTON
ADVERTISEMENT FOR
BOX MAKER, 1935
ARTIST: FRANCISCO SANS

farmacia y

A year before the 1925 *Exposition des Arts Décoratifs et Industriels Modernes* opened in Paris, the participating nations, of which Spain was one, were asked to exhibit their most stylish wares. Among those products commonly displayed in such exhibitions, cosmetic and perfume packages were best suited for Art Deco makeovers. Prior to the introduction of the German rationalist aesthetic, Deco was purely an elegant mannerism that was, as Rafael Doménech wrote, "gay and full of life, calculated to attract the spectator . . . and never vulgar" (*Commercial Art*, 1927.) Since Deco was the perfect style to sell fragrances, soaps, and powders, which already possessed mythic properties, the streamlined Deco woman was the ideal mascot for such ephemeral products. As the advertisement for Pigaline (page 319) suggests, Deco was a mask that gave its wearer instant allure. Likewise, packages with commonplace ingredients were disguised under eclectic decoration that was designed to hypnotize the buyer into believing the product had magical attributes. Most razor blades came in tiny poster-like wrappings that took the edge off and warmed up the cold steel, a sharp contrast from the mundane packages from the past. Even products that had not undergone graphic transformations, like Lejia Fénix (page 327), benefited from being framed by a counter display that exuded an Art Deco exuberance.

perfumería

(PREVIOUS PAGE)
JUNGLA
CATALOG COVER, 1935
DESIGNER: EDUARD JENER

NERVIÓN
HAIRPIN PACKAGE, 1927
ARTIST UNKNOWN

UN RUBOR
POWDER PACKAGE, 1933
ARTIST: EDUARD JENER

MADERAS DE ORIENTE
POWDER PACKAGE, 1933
ARTIST: EDUARD JENER

CREMA ELAS
TRADEMARK FOR
BEAUTY CREAM, 1933
DESIGNER UNKNOWN

RYM
ADVERTISEMENT
FOR SOAP, 1929
ARTIST UNKNOWN

BOB
SOAP BOTTLE, C. 1926
ARTIST UNKNOWN

KARAKU
BROCHURE, C. 1928
ARTIST UNKNOWN

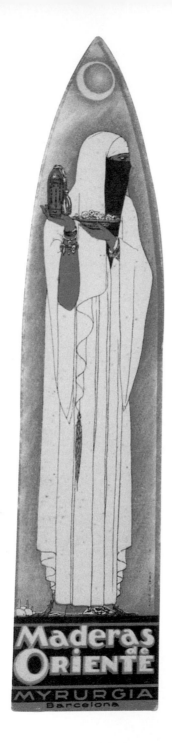

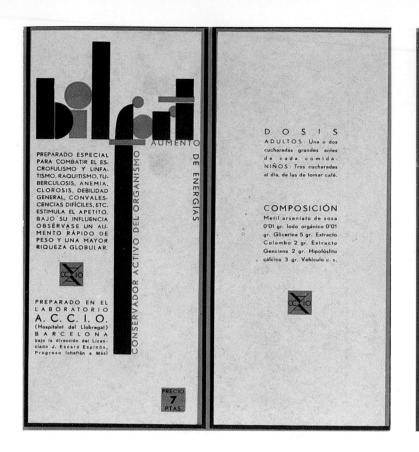

BILFORT

PACKAGE DESIGN, 1932

DESIGNER UNKNOWN

RICIL

PACKAGE DESIGN, 1932

DESIGNER UNKNOWN

AZUL MONTSERRAT
LABEL, C. 1933
DESIGNER UNKNOWN

DEPILATORIO
PACKAGE DESIGN, 1932
DESIGNER UNKNOWN

GEROBIL

PER AL DRENATGE MÈDIC DE LES VIES BILIARS

MAGNUS

GEROBIL
ADVERTISEMENT FOR
MEDICINE, C. 1933
ARTIST: RICARD
GIRALT-MIRACLE

MAGNUS
BROCHURE FOR MEDICAL
COMPANY, C. 1932
ARTIST: RICARD
GIRALT-MIRACLE

SUPERFIL
RAZOR-BLADE
PACKAGE, C. 1930
ARTIST UNKNOWN

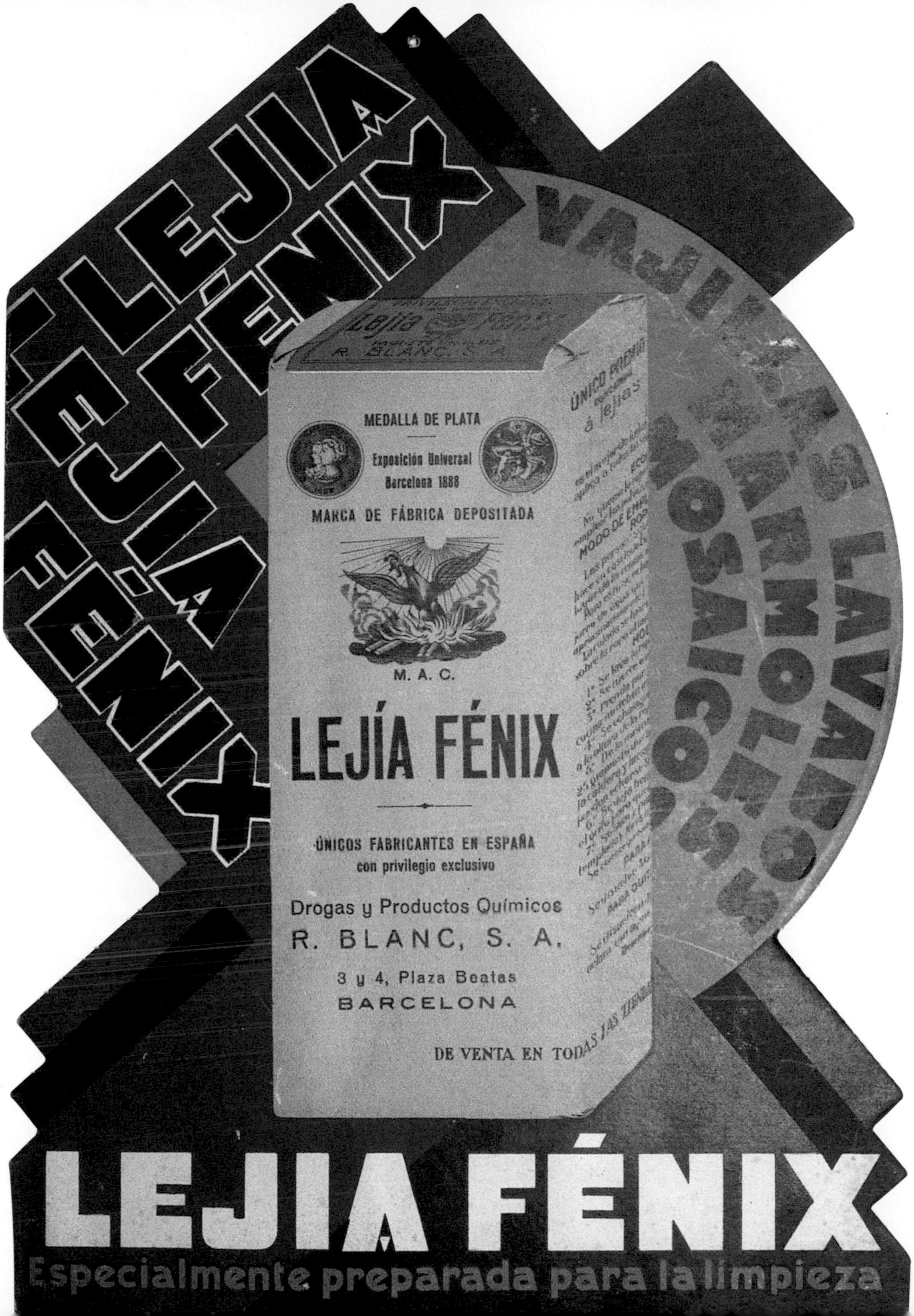

LEJÍA FÉNIX
COUNTER DISPLAY,
C. 1930
ARTIST UNKNOWN

alimentación

Food and drink can be wrapped in plain paper and clear bottles and still appeal to a consumer; but in the 1920s and 1930s, competition between Spain's leading distributors forced them to revisit the packaging and branding conventions that prevailed at that time. Fruit growers had a long tradition of designing protective wrappers, and when Art Deco came to Spain these prosaic coverlets were enlivened with contemporary graphics. For other consumables, foreign designers were commissioned to create packages and advertisements, like the sign for Pomona (page 331) that was produced by Alliance Graphique in Paris. Spain had a poster tradition dating back to the late nineteenth century, particularly for wines and liquors, but the posters were primarily images with lettering put in as an afterthought. The Art Deco aesthetic required a seamless marriage of type and image, as in the advertisement for Laponia (page 329). Tobacco, one of Europe's most popular staples, was probably the biggest beneficiary of Deco styling. During the 1920s, a large number of brands were released, each with distinctive designs. Although posters advertised brands, the packages themselves were designed to capture the buyer's loyalty. Ideales (page 334) was the most popular of the lot, but the package for Campeones with its metallic wrapper and heroic graphics is the epitome of Art Deco marketing.

y tabacos

LAPONIA
POSTER, C. 1930
ARTIST: CATALOJ

PONCHE PARERA

LABEL, C. 1930

DESIGNER UNKNOWN

DESTILERIAS: H. DE J. PARERA BARCELONA
FUNDADAS EN 1866

VARIOUS BOTTLE CAPS

1930s

DESIGNERS UNKNOWN

331

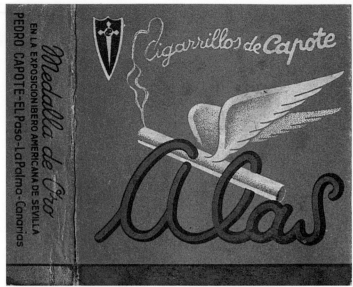

IDEALES

CIGARETTE PACKAGE, C. 1930

ARTIST: C. VIVES

LA FLOR DE LA ISABELA

LOGO FOR CIGARETTES, C. 1928

DESIGNER UNKNOWN

ALAS

CIGARETTE PACKAGE, C. 1934

DESIGNER UNKNOWN

OBRA

NEWSLETTER, 1935

DESIGNER UNKNOWN

(OPPOSITE)

CAMPEONES

CIGARETTE PACKAGE, C. 1928

ARTIST UNKNOWN

tipografía

Some critics have argued that Art Deco was decadent and senseless, while others see it for what it was, a language of design that was both a fashionable style and a vernacular idiom. In the realms of typography and type design, the introduction of basic Art Deco mannerisms in the early 1920s had the effect of grabbing the consumer's visual attention away from products and services represented by conventional or archaic styles. Although comparatively few new—or internationally popular— typefaces originated in Spain, designers customized many of the au courant alphabets for Spanish use. As a rule the Spanish type foundries, of which there were quite a few, imported existing faces from the leading foundries and distributors in France, Germany, and England; yet this was also a period when designers sought out novelty and imbued it with a modicum of individuality. Many of the most emblematic letterforms on posters and brochures were drawn by hand, based on foreign models, and given idiosyncratic personalities. Decorative tendencies from France and rationalist ideas from Germany were wed to letters that used geometry as a curiously eccentric trope. Sans serif *A*s that looked like pyramids, *E*s as circles with quarters carved away, and *F*s that seemed to be inverted stairsteps were among the frequent seen motifs. Deco alphabets ran the gamut from rococo (the cover for Comunicaciones, page 337) to Modern (advertisement for the designer J. Morell, page 341), with a range of carnival effects in between. Type, more than any other graphic element, expressed the Deco España aesthetic and signified the era in which it reigned.

COMUNICACIONES
CATALOG COVER,
C. 1930
ARTIST: BALTASAR

ADAM
BOOK TITLE, C. 1931
ARTIST: E. TROCHUT
BACHMANN

NÚMERO 3
ARCHIVOS DOCUMENTARIOS DE ARTE MODERNO

CAPITOL CINEMA
LETTERHEAD, C. 1930
DESIGNER UNKNOWN

capitol
empresa montan, s. a.
cinema
paseo recoletos, n.º 25 - madrid

LAORGA S.A.
TRADEMARK, C. 1932
DESIGNER UNKNOWN

LAORGA S.A.
MADRID

FIANDES LA
CATALUNYA DEL NORD
BOOK COVER, 1932
DESIGNER UNKNOWN

EL FARO
NEWSLETTER, 1932
DESIGNER UNKNOWN

ASMANTINA

ASMANTINA
LOGO, C. 1933
DESIGNER UNKNOWN

(OPPOSITE)
UNA FIRMA
INTERNACIONAL
DESIGNER'S
BROCHURE, C. 1930
DESIGNER: J. MORELL

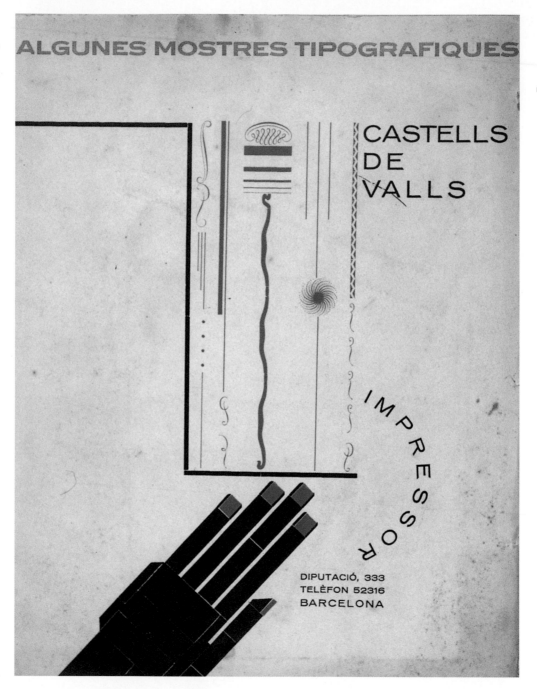

ALGUNES MOSTRES TIPOGRAFIQUES

CASTELLS
DE
VALLS

IMPRESSOR

DIPUTACIÓ, 333
TELÈFON 52316
BARCELONA

AVENIDA GAUDÍ 99

TELEFONO 55336

BARCELONA

UNA
FIRMA
INTERNACIONAL

BARCELONA

HA CREADO 280 CARTELES
HA OBTENIDO 50 PREMIOS

EN CONCURSOS NACIONALES E INTERNACIONALES

morell

CARTELES

SALÓN IDEAL

BUSINESS CARD, C. 1932

DESIGNER: E. DOGWILER

JOYAS BONAL

BUSINESS CARD, C. 1932

DESIGNER: E. DOGWILER

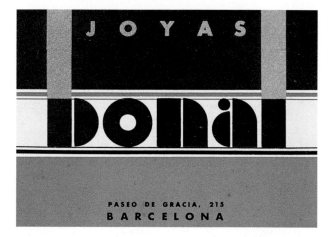

VALOR S.A.

BUSINESS CARD, C. 1932

DESIGNER: E. DOGWILER

FUMISTERIA CAÑAMERAS

ADVERTISEMENT

FOR STOVES, 1930

ARTIST: J. SALA

JOSEP RIBAS

ADVERTISEMENT

FOR FURNITURE, 1930

ARTIST: J. SALA

MUNDO GRAFICO

MAGAZINE LOGO, 1928

DESIGNER UNKNOWN

ALFABETOS

CLASICOS Y

MODERNOS

20 LAMINAS

EN COLOR

2.ª EDICIÓN

libreria · ediciones · de arte · barcelona

ABCDEFG
HIJKLMNO
PQRSTUVX
YZ. AMNS

PUBLI CINEMA

TRADEMARK, C. 1930

DESIGNER UNKNOWN

RIESGO FILM

TRADEMARK, C. 1935

DESIGNER UNKNOWN

ADAM

CATALOG COVER, C. 1931

ARTIST: E. TROCHUT

BACHMANN

ARCHIVO DOCUMENTARIO DE ARTE MODERNO

PARA EL ESTUDIO Y LA MODERNIZACION RACIONAL DEL ARTE TIPOGRAFICO

346

1932

NEW YEAR'S CARD, 1931

ARTIST: RICHARD

GIRALT-MIRACLE

VALLS

POSTER STAMP, 1931

DESIGNER UNKNOWN

"LOS CLAVELES"

TRADEMARK, C. 1923

DESIGNER UNKNOWN

DU°

MOD

IN THE 1920s, WHEN THE INDUSTRIALIZED WORLD ENTERED A MACHINE AGE, AN ELEGANT, STREAMLINED STYLE KNOWN AS ART MODERNE WAS ADOPTED BY DESIGNERS IN EUROPE, NORTH AMERICA, AND ASIA AND APPLIED TO ARCHITECTURE, FURNITURE, JEWELRY, CLOTHING, AND GRAPHICS. **INTRODUCTION** THIS WAS THE SECOND TIME IN THE TWENTIETH CENTURY THAT A DESIGN LANGUAGE PROLIFERATED THROUGHOUT THE WORLD WITH SUCH UBIQUITY — THE FIRST WIDESPREAD STYLE WAS ART NOUVEAU, WHICH BEGAN IN THE 1890s AND ENDED BEFORE WORLD WAR I. ALLOWING FOR CERTAIN INDIGENOUS VARIATIONS IN EACH OF THE NATIONS WHERE IT TOOK HOLD, ART MODERNE BECAME THE DOMINANT INTERNATIONAL DESIGN STYLE BETWEEN THE WORLD WARS. AN ORIGINAL SYNTHESIS OF CUBISM AND ANCIENT EGYPTIAN AND MAYAN DESIGN MOTIFS, ART MODERNE SPREAD THROUGHOUT POST-WORLD WAR I FRANCE, GERMANY, ENGLAND, ITALY, AND EASTERN EUROPE BEFORE EMERGING IN HOLLAND.

THIS BOOK EXAMINES HOW ART MODERNE (ALSO CALLED MODERNISTIC) GRAPHIC DESIGN WAS MANIFEST IN THE NETHERLANDS IN THE 1920s AND 1930s. ALTHOUGH DUTCH DESIGNERS DID NOT INVENT THE STYLE, THEY CERTAINLY HELPED TO POPULARIZE IT. AND WHILE THERE IS NOTHING INHERENTLY DUTCH ABOUT ART MODERNE, DUTCH DESIGNERS AND MERCHANTS ENTHUSIASTICALLY EMBRACED IT, NOT AS A RADICAL FORMAL LANGUAGE, BUT AS AN ALTERNATIVE TO BOTH TRADITIONAL AND REVOLUTIONARY GRAPHIC APPROACHES.

AS A MARKETING TOOL, ART MODERNE, WITH ITS STREAMLINED AESTHETIC, WAS SUITED TO AN INTERNATIONAL COMMERCIAL CULTURE THAT STRESSED THE IMAGE OF PROGRESS

BROOD KOEK EN BANKET BAKKERIJ

DE ONDERNEMING

OVER THE LEGACY OF THE PAST. ART AND INDUSTRY WERE ALLIED IN A CRUSADE TO CHANGE THE POPULAR PERCEPTION OF BUSINESS FROM STODGY TO VITAL. AND ART MODERNE EPITOMIZED WHAT THE INDUSTRIAL DESIGNER RAYMOND LOWEY REFERRED TO IN THE 1930s AS MAYA, "MOST ADVANCED YET ACCEPTABLE," AN ETHIC OF PURPOSEFULLY GRADUAL CHANGE. COMPARED TO THE EPITOME OF PROGRESSIVISM — THE COLD FUNCTIONALITY OF EUROPEAN MODERNIST MOVEMENTS SUCH AS THE BAUHAUS, PURISM, AND CONSTRUCTIVISM — ART MODERNE OFFERED A BALANCE OF ELEGANCE AND SIMPLICITY. IT WAS THEREFORE NOT A REVOLUTION IN DESIGN BUT AN EVOLUTION, FROM THE CURVILINEAR DECORATIVE STYLE THAT WAS ART NOUVEAU TO A RECTILINEAR ONE IN WHICH SHARP GEOMETRIES WERE THE HALLMARK OF MACHINE-BASED RATHER THAN ORGANIC AESTHETICS.

GIVEN HOLLAND'S SMALL SIZE AND POPULATION ITS CONTRIBUTION TO TWENTIETH-CENTURY AVANT-GARDE TYPOGRAPHY, PHOTOGRAPHY, AND GRAPHICS HAS BEEN DISPROPORTIONATELY PROFOUND. AFTER WORLD WAR I DUTCH DESIGNERS AND TYPOGRAPHERS AGGRESSIVELY CHALLENGED THE STATUS QUO BY TESTING THE LIMITS OF CONVENTIONAL VISUAL COMMUNICATION. TWO DISTINCT MOVEMENTS DEVELOPED, ONE ECLECTIC, THE OTHER ASCETIC. THE ECLECTIC STYLE WAS A DECORATIVE EXPRESSIONIST AESTHETIC ALTERNATELY REFERRED TO AS THE WENDINGEN STYLE, AFTER THE MAGAZINE OF THE SAME NAME, MEANING TURN OR UPHEAVAL, OR THE WIJDEVELD STYLE, SO NAMED FOR ITS INVENTOR, THE ARCHITECT, DESIGNER, AND EDITOR, H. TH. WIJDEVELD. IN 1918 HE FOUNDED WENDINGEN, THE JOURNAL OF A LOOSELY KNIT GROUP OF EXPRESSIONISTS KNOWN AS THE AMSTERDAM SCHOOL.

The second movement was the purist ethic of De Stijl (The Style), founded in 1917 by Theo van Doesburg who edited its journal of the same name. It was a reaction to the chaotic nature of art and design at the time, and an unprecedented rationalist methodology based on formalist experiments in architecture and visual communications that was destined to influence design throughout Europe.

The Wendingen style, writes Paolo Portoghesi in his book Wendingen, was known for "irrationality, perception through vision; De Stijl was known for rationality, perception through analysis" (Portoghesi and Fanelli, 1988). The Wendingen style was tied to a past era by its extravagances, which included complex and artful typographics. De Stijl was dedicated to a utopian future that rejected extravagance for economy. Despite these differences both schools did agree that an upheaval of values was necessary before society could be reoriented and reshaped.

Initially this proposition was presented by Holland's most influential architect, H. P. Berlage, who as early as 1903 began Holland's artistic renewal through the concept of "honesty in construction." In a critique of the nineteenth-century ornamental excesses that were still being affixed to architecture and graphics in the Netherlands he wrote, "The sham art has to be fought. We wish for reality again and not phantoms." Berlage advocated that design of all kinds should serve the community spiritually as well as functionally.

Although those who were influenced by Berlage shared this goal, they nevertheless developed his idea to extremes. "De Stijl exasperated the theme of formal simplification and rationality, and attained an absolute abstraction," wrote the German critic and architect Erich Mendelsohn in 1920. "The Amsterdam school exasperated the expressive search, the plastic characterization, the individualism, and adopted and developed many stylistic elements typical of the maestro [Berlage] but with a new accent that abandoned [him]" (quoted in Portoghesi and Fanelli, 1988).

In their attempt to alter popular perception by transforming traditional Dutch aesthetics, Wendingen artists introduced approaches that were often too artfully convoluted, while De Stijl was too rigidly mathematical. Wijdeveld was obsessed with the close unity of text and decoration in which legibility was not as important as graphic nuance or gesture. Geometric letter forms made from the lead slugs used in letterpress printing were run together without letter or word spacing. The effect was visually harmonious out sometimes illegible. Wijdeveld's typographic work received sporadic attention "mixed with irritation and jealousy. Irritation mostly for the presumed illegibility.... Jealousy for Wendingen's joyous aggressiveness," wrote Giovanni Fanelli in his essay "Wendingen as a Model of Typographic Art" (Portoghesi and Fanelli, 1988).

Van Doesburg and his early colleagues, among them the painter Piet Mondrian

AND ARCHITECTS J. J. P. OUD AND GERRIT RIETVELD, AIMED AT EXPRESSING THE UNIVERSAL PRINCIPLE OF TOTAL ABSTRACTION, OR WHAT H. L. C. JAFFÉ IN DE STIJL 1917-1931 CALLS "A RENDERING OF EXACT AND EQUILIBRIATED RELATIONS" THAT RESULTED IN COOL, ANALYTICAL DESIGN FORMS (JAFFÉ, 1986). DE STIJL WAS AGGRESSIVE IN ITS ORDERLINESS AND PRECISION. BY EMBRACING STRICT MODERNIST FORMALISM AND SOCIAL UTOPIANISM, DE STIJL WAS DEVOTED TO WHAT JAFFÉ CALLS THE "COLLECTIVE IMPERSONAL STYLE," A SEARCH FOR THE PLATONIC IDEAL.

CONTEMPORARY CRITICS, AND MANY CLIENTS, WERE ALIENATED BY BOTH SCHOOLS' REJECTION OF CONVENTIONAL AESTHETICS. YET SINCE THE WENDINGEN STYLE AND DE STIJL WERE PRACTICED FOR A DECADE AND A HALF, THEY EXERTED A PROFOUND STYLISTIC AND FORMAL INFLUENCE ON DUTCH COMMERCIAL GRAPHIC DESIGN. IN ADDITION TO HIS WORK ON WENDINGEN, WIJDEVELD PROMOTED HIS TYPOGRAPHY THROUGH DESIGNS FOR BOOKS AND CULTURAL POSTERS; THE STYLE WAS ADOPTED BY FOLLOWERS AND INNOVATORS WORKING IN SIMILAR MEDIA. VAN DOESBURG AND THE OTHER LOOSELY KNIT DE STIJL MEMBERS WHO PRACTICED GRAPHIC DESIGN ALSO MAINTAINED A VISUAL PRESENCE IN THE COMMERCIAL WORLD THROUGH ADVERTISING AND PACKAGES FOR MANUFACTURERS AND MERCHANTS. MOREOVER, VAN DOESBURG WAS INTERNATIONALLY RENOWNED FOR HIS RELATIONSHIP WITH OTHER MODERN MOVEMENTS INCLUDING CONSTRUCTIVISM, DADA, AND A RATHER CONTENTIOUS SOJOURN AT THE BAUHAUS. BY THE EARLY 1920S THE IDEAS PROMOTED BY BOTH SCHOOLS HAD INSPIRED OTHER DESIGNERS TO SERIOUSLY ADDRESS THE PAUCITY OF

SOPHISTICATED COMMERCIAL GRAPHIC DESIGN IN HOLLAND AS COMPARED TO OTHER INDUSTRIALIZED EUROPEAN NATIONS.

ALTHOUGH AN ACTIVE MOVEMENT OF DUTCH DESIGNERS REEVALUATED AND REVIVED CLASSIC TYPOGRAPHY, THEY WERE CONCERNED WITH REESTABLISHING THE TRADITIONS LOST DURING THE LATTER PART OF THE NINETEENTH CENTURY, WHEN THE GRAPHIC ARTS WERE AT THEIR NADIR. FOLLOWERS OF THE WENDINGEN STYLE AND DE STIJL WERE MORE INTERESTED IN CHANGING THOSE NICETIES. DESPITE THE IMPRESSIVE REFORMS OF THE TRADITIONALISTS, GRAPHIC DESIGN IN THE NETHERLANDS DURING THE 1920S WAS PUSHED IN THE DIRECTION OF TWO GRAPHIC STYLES: MODERN AND MODERNISTIC. THE FORMER WAS INFLUENCED BY EUROPE'S AVANT-GARDE, AND THE LATTER BY EUROPE'S DOMINANT COMMERCIAL STYLE.

BEFORE DISCUSSING DUTCH ART MODERNE, IT IS NECESSARY TO UNDERSTAND THE IMPACT OF AND RESPONSE TO THE MODERN MOVEMENT, FOR IT BOTH THREATENED AND REVIVED DUTCH COMMERCIAL CULTURE AND HAD BOTH A POSITIVE AND NEGATIVE INFLUENCE ON THE MODERNISTIC DESIGN. BEGINNING IN THE EARLY 1920S MODERN DESIGN MADE INROADS THROUGH THE EFFORTS OF SEMINAL DESIGNERS SUCH AS PIET ZWART, PAUL SCHUITEMA, GERARD KILJAN, WIM BRUSSE, HENNY CAHAN, AND DICK ELFFERS, WHO PRACTICED A VARIANT OF CONSTRUCTIVISM THAT INVOLVED ASYMMETRIC TYPOGRAPHY, PRIMARY COLORS, AND PHOTOMONTAGE. BY THE MID-1930S, OVER A DECADE AFTER RUSSIAN CONSTRUCTIVISM AND THE NEW TYPOGRAPHY (THE FUNCTIONAL TYPOGRAPHIC SYSTEM CODIFIED IN GERMANY BY JAN TSCHICOLD IN HIS BOOK NEUE TYPOGRAPHIE) HAD PEAKED AS VIABLE

DESIGN METHODOLOGIES, DUTCH CONSTRUCTIVISM AND TYPO-FOTO, AS THE MARRIAGE OF TYPE AND MONTAGE WAS CALLED, WERE ACCEPTED AS ADVERTISING CONVENTIONS BY VARIOUS CULTURAL, BUSINESS, AND GOVERNMENT INSTITUTIONS. THE PTT (THE DUTCH POSTAL, TELEPHONE, AND TELEGRAPH COMPANY) BLAZED A TRAIL FOR PROGRESSIVE DESIGN BY COMMISSIONING PIET ZWART, AMONG OTHER MODERNS, TO CREATE MATERIALS THAT ARE PARADIGMS OF THE ERA'S FUNCTIONAL AESTHETIC. PRAISE WAS ALSO HEARD IN THE DESIGN INDUSTRY FOR NEW, RATIONALIST APPROACHES, AS WERE ARGUMENTS THAT EMPHASIZED THE CREATION OF NEW STANDARDS OF BEAUTY AS AN ALTERNATIVE TO OUTDATED FORMS. AND YET CRITICISM FOR THESE APPROACHES CONTINUED.

ANTIQUATED APPROACHES HAD DOMINATED DUTCH GRAPHICS EVEN AS EUROPEAN DESIGN WAS CHANGING BY LEAPS AND BOUNDS. PRIOR TO WORLD WAR I THE NETHERLANDS WAS NOT KNOWN FOR A HIGH LEVEL OF GRAPHIC OR ADVERTISING DESIGN. DESPITE THE ANOMALY OF A FEW BEAUTIFUL POSTERS IN THE POSTIMPRESSIONIST, SYMBOLIST, MAGIC REALIST, AND EXPRESSIONIST STYLES, HOLLAND'S COMMERCIAL GRAPHICS FAR FROM EQUALED THE INNOVATIVE POSTERS, LETTERING, AND TYPOGRAPHY OF FIN-DE-SIECLE FRANCE, GERMANY, ENGLAND, AND ITALY. LEADERS OF INDUSTRY AND GOVERNMENT IN THOSE CONSUMER NATIONS REALIZED THE BENEFITS OF JOINING ART WITH INDUSTRY, BUT THEIR DUTCH COUNTERPARTS RESISTED ENTRUSTING ARTISTS WITH MATTERS OF COMMERCE. WHILE ARCHITECTURE WAS EXPERIENCING A RENAISSANCE OF SORTS, GRAPHICS WERE KEPT LOCKED IN A TIME WARP. ADVERTISING AGENCIES EXISTED, BUT MOST ENCOURAGED MEDIOC-

J.W. DE GONJE
Wallpaper Manufacturer's Neon Sign, 1935
Roel Knobbe

RITY AS ADVERTISERS RAILED AGAINST THE "ARTISTIC DESIGNER" FOR BEING AN AESTHETE WHO DID NOT UNDERSTAND THE CONVENTIONS OF MARKETING.

YET THE ADVERTISER'S NEGATIVE ATTITUDE AND THE RESULTING AESTHETIC STAGNATION CANNOT BE BLAMED ENTIRELY ON AN IRRATIONAL MISTRUST OF AESTHETES, FOR THE DEEPLY ROOTED CALVINISM INSTILLED EVEN IN NON-PROTESTANTS INSPIRED A FUNDAMENTAL DISTASTE FOR MARKETING OF ANY KIND. ADVERTISING WAS CONSIDERED A SINFUL MEDIUM. HOLLAND'S LATE DEVELOPMENT OF AN INDIGENOUS VISUAL CULTURE CAN THEREFORE BE ATTRIBUTED TO THE BELIEF THAT ADVERTISING WAS A NECESSARY EVIL, AND THUS UNENTHUSIASTICALLY SUPPORTED BY THE VERY BUSINESS PEOPLE WHO NEEDED IT MOST. AS DICK DOOIJES AND PIETER BRATTINGA EXPLAIN, "IN LEADING CIRCLES IN THE NETHERLANDS MONEY HAS A DIRTY NAME AND IS NOT TO BE TALKED ABOUT. IT WAS THEREFORE VERY HARD FOR THESE PEOPLE TO APPRECIATE THE ARTISTS WHO WERE WILLING TO PUT THEIR 'GOD-GIVEN' TALENTS AT THE DISPOSAL OF MONEYMAKERS" (DOOIJES AND BRATTINGA, 1968).

THE PLAN OF HOLLAND'S CITIES ALSO CONTRIBUTED TO THE LATE START OF DUTCH GRAPHIC DESIGN, PARTICULARLY THE POSTER. UNLIKE MOST EUROPEAN CAPITALS, WHERE POSTERS WERE HUNG ALONG THE GRAND BOULEVARDS AND WIDE AVENUES, DUTCH CITIES ARE WEBS OF SMALL WINDING STREETS. THE DUTCH POSTER WAS THEREFORE NOT DESIGNED FOR LONG-DISTANCE VIEWING, WITH STARK COLORS AND SIMPLE IMAGES, BUT WAS MORE TYPE HEAVY, FOR SHORT-DISTANCE READING.

ALTHOUGH IN THE LATE NINETEENTH CENTURY SOME HISTORICALLY SIGNIFICANT

ATTEMPTS WERE MADE TO ELEVATE GRAPHICS BY ADOPTING THE TENETS OF ART NOUVEAU (NIEUWE KUNST IN DUTCH), THE RESULTS DID NOT COMPARE WITH, OR AT BEST MIMICKED, FRENCH AND GERMAN APPROACHES. NOT UNTIL AFTER WORLD WAR I DID A DISTINCTIVE NATIONAL STYLE BEGIN TO SHOW ITSELF IN POSTERS BY PIONEERS SUCH AS R. N. ROLAND HOLST, C. A. LION CACHET, ALBERT PIETER HAHN, SR., JAN C. B. SLUYTERS, AND JACOB (JAC.) JONGERT. THE UNIQUE MARRIAGE OF RAW EXPRESSIONISM AND CARNIVAL-LIKE ORNAMENTALISM NOT ONLY REFLECTED THE STYLISTIC AND CONCEPTUAL FLUX WITHIN CONTEMPORARY ART BUT SYMBOLIZED THE CATHARTIC EFFECTS OF THE WAR.

THE HORRORS OF WORLD WAR I INEXORABLY ALTERED BASIC HUMAN VALUES AND USHERED IN NEW VISUAL EXPRESSIONS. WHILE IN NEIGHBORING EUROPEAN COUNTRIES MONARCHIES FELL AND INSTITUTIONS CRUMBLED, IN HOLLAND WORKERS WERE EMPOWERED THROUGH THE SOCIAL DEMOCRATIC WORKERS' PARTY. GOODS AND MONEY WERE REDISTRIBUTED WHEN A PRIVATIZED SYSTEM WAS TRANSFORMED INTO A MORE DEMOCRATIC ONE. TURMOIL IN ALL SEGMENTS OF SOCIETY WAS IMPETUS ENOUGH FOR ARTISTS TO TAKE MORE CRITICAL ROLES IN POLITICS AND CULTURE. THE WENDINGEN STYLE AND DE STIJL CERTAINLY WERE SPUN OUT OF THIS VORTEX OF CHANGE. ARTISTS ACTIVELY INVOLVED THEMSELVES BY DESIGNING POLITICAL PROPAGANDA IN AN ATTEMPT TO FIND NEW AVENUES FOR THEIR GRAPHIC VOCABULARIES.

TRADE ORGANIZATIONS WERE FOUNDED TO ADVOCATE GREATER PARTICIPATION OF ARTISTS IN DUTCH SOCIETY. AND AS THE NEW PROFESSION OF ARTIST-DESIGNER GAINED A

DE MEIDOORN

NATUURHISTORIES MAANDBLAD VOOR BUITEN-
VRIENDEN ONDER REDAKTIE VAN HENK VAN LAAR

Uitg. AJC, Reguliersgracht 78 Amsterdam - Tel 30691
Postrekening 54638, Abonnementsprys F. 1.- per halfjaar,
by vooruitbetaling - Losse Nrs 20 ct.

DE MEIDOORN
Masthead for nature magazine,
1931

FOOTHOLD IN POSTWAR HOLLAND, PRESSURE WAS PUT ON THE GOVERNMENT AND INDUSTRY

TO USE GOOD DESIGN. YET THE DEFINITION OF WHAT WAS GOOD (OR APPROPRIATE) DESIGN

BECAME A POINT OF CONTENTION. PROGRESSIVE ARTISTS AND THEIR PATRONS STRUGGLED

TO CREATE STANDARDS BASED ON CONTEMPORARY VALUES, SUCH AS ELEMENTARISM AND

FUNCTIONALISM. NEVERTHELESS, A COUNTERFORCE FROM ADVERTISING AND BUSINESS

ARGUED AGAINST THE NEW FORMS AS ABERRATIONS.

SOMEWHERE BETWEEN THE OLD TRADITION OF A CRAFTSMAN-ARTIST LOYAL TO PAST

VERITIES AND THE NEW IDEA OF AN ARTIST-ENGINEER DEVOTED TO THE MOST ELEMENTAL

METHODS OF VISUAL COMMUNICATION IS FOUND THE PRACTITIONER OF ART MODERNE, WHO

PROFFERED A COMPROMISE AESTHETIC THAT BALANCED DECORATIVE ART WITH MODERN THE-

ORY. BUT ART MODERNE WAS NOT INVENTED IN HOLLAND, ART MODERNE WAS IMPORTED

FROM FRANCE AND GERMANY. THE FRENCH MASTER A. M. CASSANDRE PROVIDED THE MOLD

FROM WHICH MANY DUTCH EXAMPLES DERIVED. THE TRADE MAGAZINES, MOST NOTABLY DE

Reclame (Advertising), which had given perfunctory coverage to the New Typography, extolled the virtues of art moderne through covers and articles that exhibited the best European and Dutch stylists.

As elsewhere in Europe, art moderne in Holland was exuberant, though politically neutral. While the New Typography was symbolic of socialist, communist, or utopian ideals (even as applied to certain mainstream industries), art moderne represented the fashion and trend of the moment. As a universal style it was inoffensive in the mass marketplace, whether promoting products or ideas, and could be used effectively for a variety of purposes.

Despite this symbolic neutrality, art moderne did develop a distinct idiom incorporating typographic characteristics of the Wendingen style, De Stijl, and the New Typography. Art moderne, although downplayed in accounts of Dutch graphic design, evolved from a synthesis of traditional and radical forms into a viable commercial language that enjoyed popularity, peaked in the 1930s, and almost completely disappeared during World War II when the hardships of occupation eliminated the need for vigorous commercial advertising. After the war, art moderne was played out in Holland, replaced by both nondescript forms and the Swiss-inspired international style. Although art moderne is obsolete today, gone without a trace from current graphic design in the Netherlands, it was the means by which the Dutch avant-garde was assimilated and demystified.

For centuries the Netherlands has been a haven of free speech. During the eighteenth century, Dutch artists created reams of acerbic social and satiric prints, which were freely distributed and served as archetypes for other European artists. By the **POLITICS** early twentieth century a multitude of posters were created to promote the candidates and ideals of Holland's disproportionately numerous political parties. Comprising the political alphabet soup were, among others, RKSP (Rooms-Katholieke Staatspartij), CPN (Communist Party of the Netherlands), and SDAP (Social Democratic Workers' Party). The last, the leading Dutch labor advocate, was the most prolific producer of posters, and in the 1930s art moderne was the principal style of persuasion. Portraying the worker in stylized monumental poses helped underscore the myth of the noble proletariat that SDAP and other labor groups hoped to propagate. By the late 1920s and 1930s, when the worldwide economic depression struck the Netherlands, these graphic representations helped uplift the suffering worker's image. Yet art moderne was not monopolized by the SDAP — its opponents also effectively used the style to capture hearts and minds.

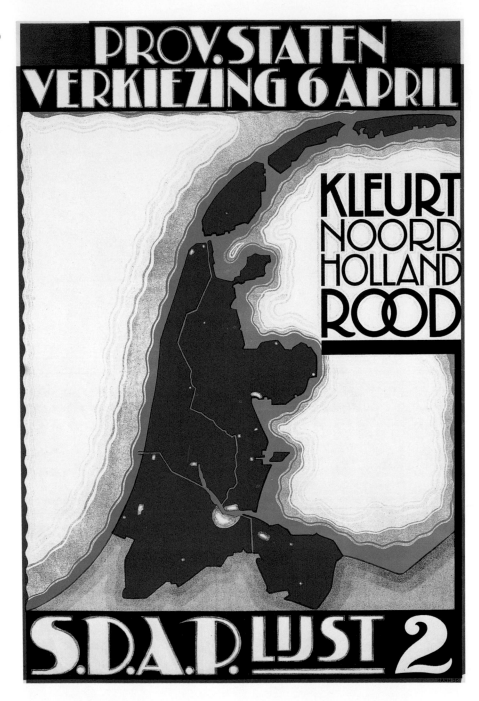

PROV. STATEN
VERKIEZING 6 APRIL

KLEURT
NOORD.
HOLLAND
ROOD

S.D.A.P. LIJST 2

WELVAARTS POLITIEK SDAP
Election poster, 1935
Huib de Ru

SPORTSLUI!
Anti-alcohol poster, 1935
Albert Pieter Hahn, Jr.

SDAP LIJST 4 WIBAUT
Election poster, c. 1927
Albert Pieter Hahn, Jr.

STEMT ROOD!
SDAP election poster, 1919
Albert Pieter Hahn, Sr.

STEMT DEN COMMUNIST
Election poster, c. 1930
J. Walter

TEGEN OORLOG
Antiwar/pension poster, 1930
Meijer Bleekrode

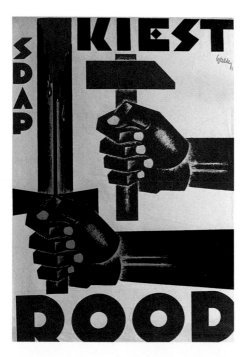

KIEST ROOD
Election poster, 1929
J. Walter

Since business and industry were initially reticent to accept avant-garde design, the cultural arena became the proving ground for change in graphic arts. Some of the most significant typographic experiments were done as exhibition announcements and for **CULTURE** book covers. Although Wendingen occasionally expressed political ideas, it was primarily a cultural journal whose impact was on the arts community and its schools. The journal was a showcase for the aesthetics that came to underscore the active cultural life of Holland. The distinctive geometric labyrinth used by the Wendingen stylists in their graphics became a virtual emblem of early postwar Dutch design. In adulterated form, the Wendingen style's rectilinear, decorative mannerisms were adopted and promoted through advertising trade magazines, which exploited the commercial advantages of this radical style. The most popular of these magazines, De Reclame, was more likely to feature decorative styles over functional modern approaches, and it gave only a modicum of attention to purist aesthetics. The covers of this influential periodical, which were usually adorned with modernistic images, served as models for print shops, advertising agencies, and the majority of ontworpers (commercial designers).

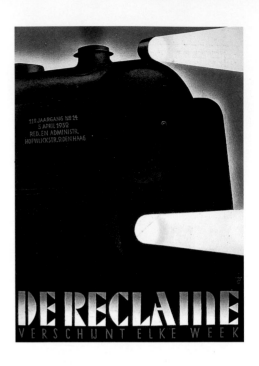

DE RECLAME
Advertising magazine cover, 1932
F. Funke

DE RECLAME
Advertising magazine cover, 1932
J. A. W. von Stein

DE RECLAME
Advertising magazine cover, 1930
Mander

DE RECLAME
Advertising magazine cover, 1932
F. Funke

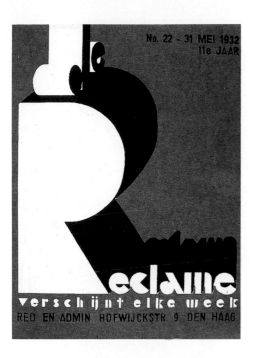

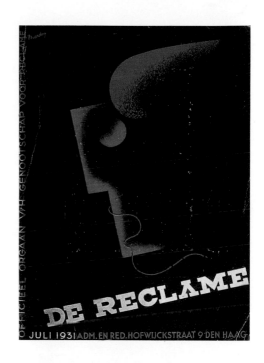

DE RECLAME
Advertising magazine cover, 1932

DE RECLAME
Advertising magazine cover, 1931
Marton

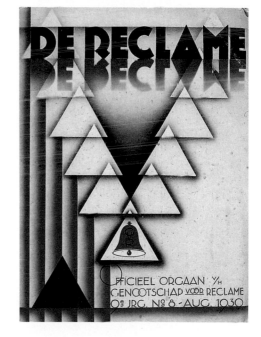

DE RECLAME
Advertising magazine cover, 1932
F. Funke

DE RECLAME
Advertising magazine cover, 1930

VAN NEDERLANDSCHE
GEMEENTE WERKEN
Exhibition poster, 1926
Antoon Kurvers

BUITENLANDSCH BIND WERK
VAN DEZEN TIJD
Exhibition poster, 1924
H. Th. Wijdeveld

MOND-EN TANDHYGIËNE
Exhibition poster, 1925

TOONEELMAAND KUNSTKRING
Exhibition poster, c. 1920
Frans ter Gast

DE ROODE DANSERES
Dance poster, 1922
Jan C. B. Sluyters

STAD MECHELEN RETROSPECTIEVE
TENTOONSTELLING
Exhibition poster, 1927
Jan Kuper

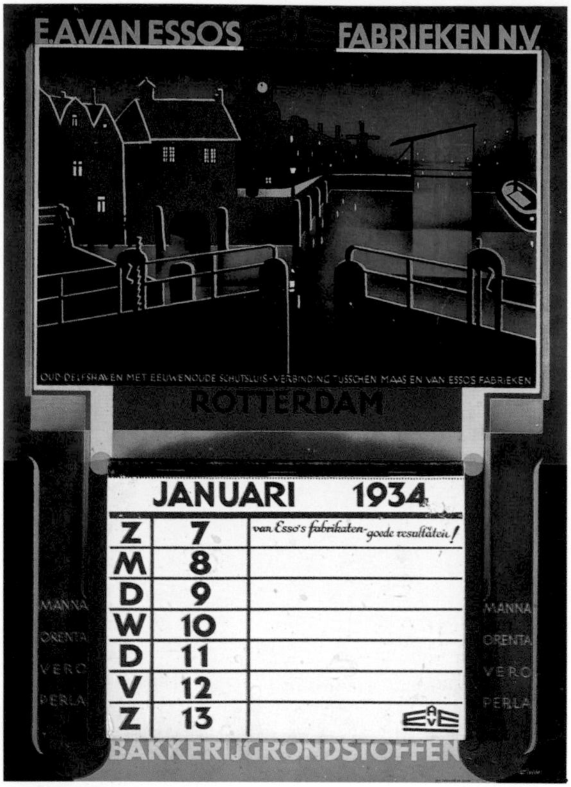
E.A. VAN ESSO'S
FABRIEKEN N.V.
OUD-DELFSHAVEN MET EEUWENOUDE SCHUTSLUIS-VERBINDING TUSSCHEN MAAS EN VAN ESSOS FABRIEKEN
ROTTERDAM
JANUARI 1934
Z 7
M 8
D 9
W 10
D 11
V 12
Z 13
van Esso's fabrikaten-goede resultaten!
MANNA
ORENTA
VERO
PERLA
BAKKERIJGRONDSTOFFEN

E.A. VAN ESSO'S
FABRIEKEN N.V.
Calendar, 1934

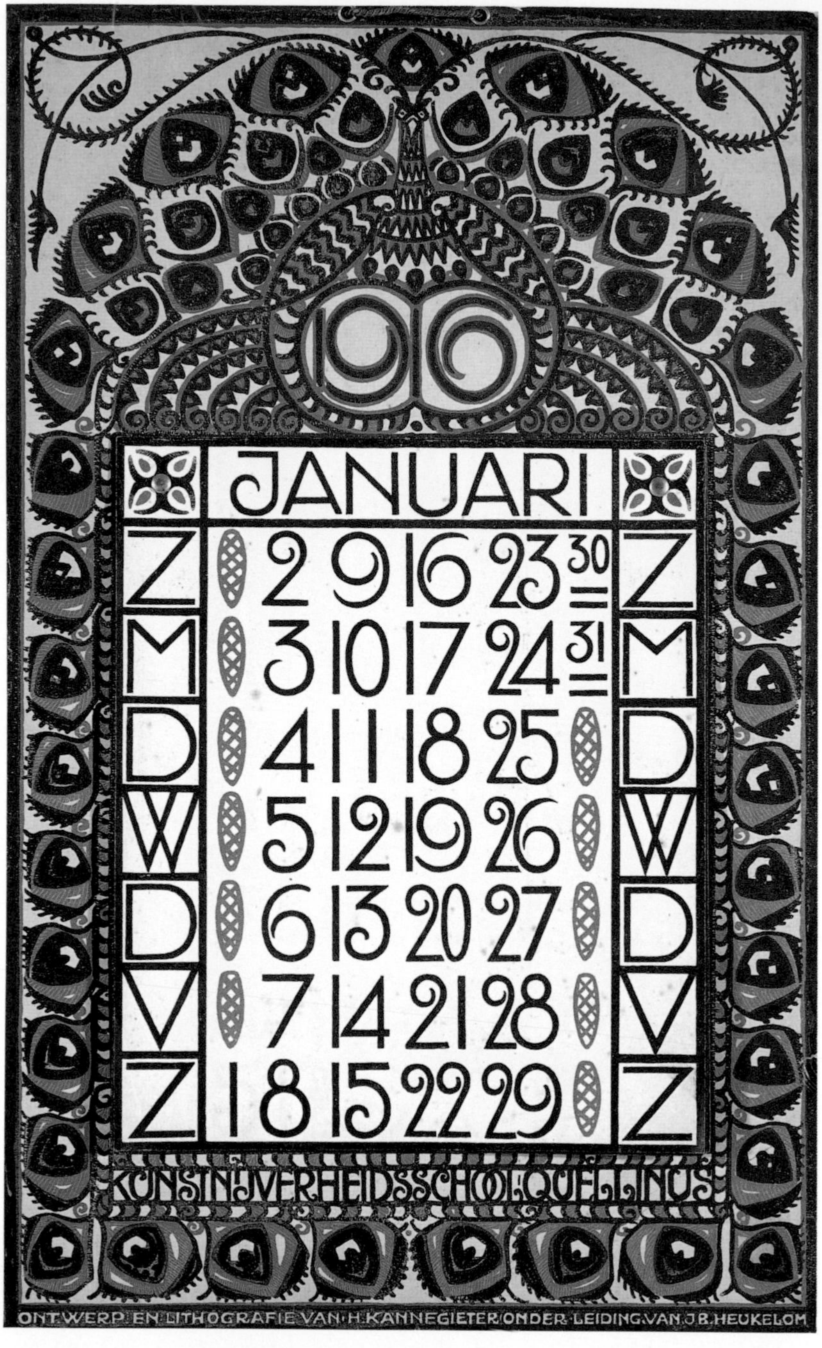
1916
JANUARI
Z 2 9 16 23 30 Z
M 3 10 17 24 31 M
D 4 11 18 25 D
W 5 12 19 26 W
D 6 13 20 27 D
V 7 14 21 28 V
Z 1 8 15 22 29 Z
KUNSTNIJVERHEIDSSCHOOL QUELLINUS
ONTWERP EN LITHOGRAFIE VAN H. KANNEGIETER ONDER LEIDING VAN J.B. HEUKELOM

1916
Calendar, 1916
Van H. Kannegieter

ULTRAPHOON HUIS
Record jackets, c. 1922
Chris Lebeau

OCTOBER, 1930
Calendar, 1930
H. Th. Wijdeveld

TENTOONSTELLING
Exhibition poster, 1925
P. A. H. Hofman

HAACISCHE KUNSTKRING
Exhibition poster, 1932
P. A. H. Hofman

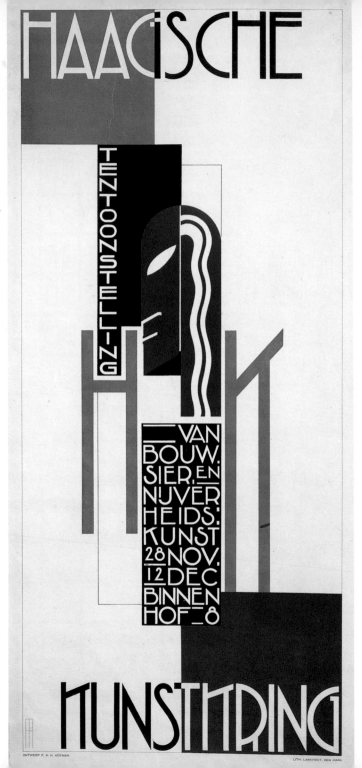

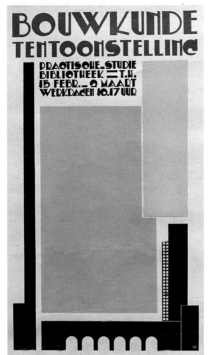

BOUWKUNDE
TENTOONSTELLING
Exhibition poster, c. 1930
H.K.

TENTOONSTELLING
Exhibition poster, 1923
Antoon Kurvers

Due to the country's deep-seated work-ethic and free-market liberalism, many international corporations were based in Holland by the twentieth century. VANK (Association of Artists of Crafts and Industry), founded in 1904, promoted the development **INDUSTRY** of arts and crafts in the industrial sector through publications, exhibitions, and demonstrations of design's benefits. During the late 1920s Holland's most progressive designers, such as Piet Zwart and Paul Schuitema, applied constructivist and rationalist typography for certain forward-looking industrial clients, but the dominant graphic style was art moderne. Despite the complaint of some design critics that art moderne was a meaningless conglomeration of printer's ornaments, it served many masters well. The industrial giant, Philips, producer of radios, lighting, and electronic parts, became one of the most visible manufacturers in Holland, and its products gained a competitive edge through the company's ambitious program of modern advertising and packaging. The annual JAARBEURS (industrial fair) in Utrecht also adopted art moderne, in striking modernistic posters that at once symbolized the future and monumentalized industry.

ECONOMIE
Rubber sole trademark, 1931

NIMCO
Shoe trademark, 1935

DUBBELGANGER
Shoe trademark, 1931

DAROELY'S SCHOENEN
Shoe advertisement, 1932
J. P. van Wees

388

H. CUVONIER
Optician's advertisement, 1933
C. J. Snoeijerbosch

JAARBEURS
UTRECHT 9-18 SEPTEMBER
1941
NIEDERLÄNDISCHE MESSE
FOIRE NEERLANDAISE

JAARBEURS UTRECHT
Exposition poster, 1929
Erna van Osselen

JAARBEURS UTRECHT
Exposition poster, 1926
Louis Kalff

JAARBEURS UTRECHT
Exposition poster, 1934

JAARBEURS UTRECHT
Exposition poster, 1934

JAARBEURS UTRECHT
Exposition poster, 1932
Zeguers

JAARBEURS UTRECHT
Exposition poster, 1934
Henri Pieck

JAARBEURS UTRECHT
Exposition poster, 1936
Henri Pieck

393

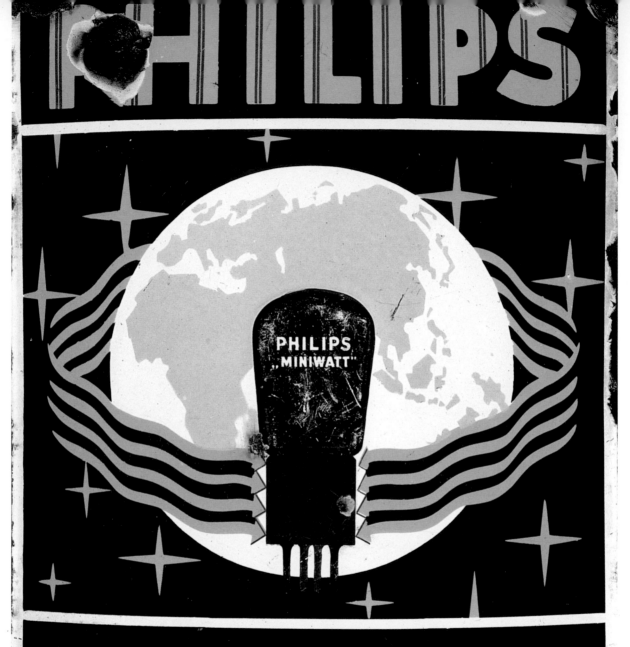

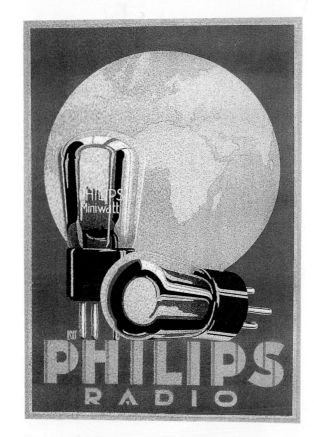

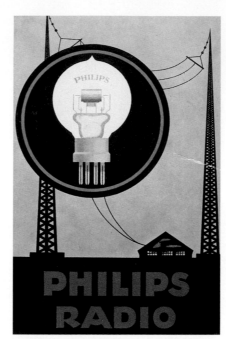

PHILIPS
Loudspeaker poster, 1930

PHILIPS
Autolight poster, c. 1920

PHILIPS

Lighting poster, c. 1940

PHILIPS

Package for film projector light, c. 1925

FOTO ARTIKELEN
Advertisement for photo supply store, 1932
W. Heijnen

FOTAX
Photo equipment trademark, 1930

PERFECTA
Magnet trademark, 1938

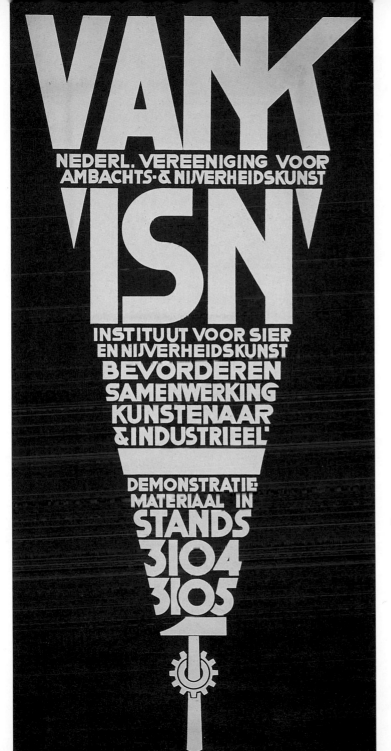

VANK
NEDERL. VEREENIGING VOOR
AMBACHTS-& NIJVERHEIDSKUNST
'ISN'
INSTITUUT VOOR SIER
EN NIJVERHEIDSKUNST
BEVORDEREN
SAMENWERKING
KUNSTENAAR
&INDUSTRIEEL'
DEMONSTRATIE
MATERIAAL IN
STANDS
3104
3105

VANK
Industrial fair poster, 1924
Nicolaas P. de Koo

HARLEKIJN SPELEN
Toy trademark, 1934

JEVEA
Motor parts trademark, 1931

ELECTROSTAR
Record company trademark, 1931

KOMUSINA
Writing machine trademark, 1930

399

SUNLIGHT ZEEP
Enamel sign for soap, 1920
M. Güthschmidth

MAAS TUNNEL
Radio battery trademark, 1937

TRIOMPHONE
Loudspeaker trademark, 1927

NEUROKARDIN
Pharmaceutical trademark, 1921

P.A. HOUBERG DROGISTERY
Pharmaceutical trademark, 1930

MAAS TUNNEL

RADIO BATTERIJ

TRIOMPHONE

NEUROKARDIN

DROGISTERIJ HET OOSTEN

P.A. HOUBERG

ASS.APOTHEKER

FRANS HALS STR N° 2

UTRECHT

401

OF THE MANY FOODS AND BEVERAGES FOR WHICH HOLLAND IS RENOWNED, NONE IS MORE CELEBRATED THAN ITS BEERS. IT MIGHT THEREFORE BE EXPECTED THAT IN A COUNTRY OF MANY COMPETING BRANDS ADVERTISMENTS FOR THIS PRODUCT WOULD BE SUPERB, BUT SURPRISINGLY, BEER AND **FOOD & DRINK** LIQUOR PROMOTIONS WERE NOT ALWAYS WELL DONE. ONLY A FEW OF THE MAJOR BREWERIES AND DISTILLERIES TRANSCENDED THE UNIMAGINATIVE CONVENTION OF SHOWING A PRODUCT. MOST NOTABLE WAS NICOLAAS P. DE KOO'S CAMPAIGN FOR PHOENIX DORT-MUNDER BEER WHICH COMBINED TRADITIONAL ILLUSTRATION WITH MODERN TYPOGRAPHY TO FORM A REBUS. YET THE MOST DISTINCTIVE AND ADVENTURESOME CAMPAIGN WAS SEEN IN JAC. JONGERT'S POSTERS, PACK-AGING, AND ADVERTISEMENTS FOR VAN NELLE COFFEES AND TEAS WHICH PRESENT DE STIJL-INSPIRED GEOMETRY AND A PRIMARY-COLOR PALETTE WITH A MODERNISTIC SENSIBILITY. VAN NELLE WAS IN THE VANGUARD OF MODERN DESIGN: ITS PACKAGES DESIGNED IN KEEPING WITH AVANT-GARDE STYLES, BUT, EVEN MORE SIGNIFICANT, ITS GLASS-WALLED FACTORY, DESIGNED IN 1930, IS A MONUMENT TO CLASSICAL MODERNISM. REFLECTING CURRENT STYLES, MANY OTHER PRODUCTS, INCLUDING DUTCH CHOCOLATES, MILK, AND BISCUITS, WERE PACKAGED AND PROMOTED THROUGH HIGHLY DECORATIVE MODERNISTIC DESIGN, THOUGH RARELY WITH THE DEVOTION TO NUANCE OF THE VAN NELLE GRAPHICS.

SANDEMAN'S
PORT
Enamel sign for
Seagram Nederland,
1925
After Laxton Knight

LOXTON
KNIGHT

SANDEMAN'S
PORT

VAN NELLE'S CIRKEL
Coffee advertisement, c. 1930
Jac. Jongert

VAN NELLE'S GEBROKEN
Tea poster, 1929
Jac. Jongert

VAN NELLE
Coffee and tea tin, c. 1930
Jac. Jongert

VAN NELLE
Coffee and tea poster, 1931
Jac. Jongert

VAN NELLE
Coffee poster, 1931
A. M. Cassandre

VAN NELLE'S
Coffee poster, 1933
Jac. Jongert

HEINEKEN'S BIER
Beer poster, c. 1928

PHOENIX DORTMUNDER
Beer posters, c. 1928
Nicolaas P. de Koo

R M I
Dairy trademark, 1934

W A
Grocery trademark, 1936

LONNEKER
Dairy trademark, 1941

EPCO
Grocery trademark, 1938

SORBETS
Ice cream trademark, 1931
W. Heijnen

408

DRINKT MELK
Milk advertisement, 1933
W. Heijnen

Since Europe for decades has been the world's largest consumer of commercial tobacco products, it is no wonder that manufacturers of cigarettes, cigars, and pipe tobacco competed fiercely during the 1920s and 1930s. Hundreds of large and small TOBACCO companies fought for customers through advertising and promotion. Although various formats were used and virtually any style would do, art moderne perfectly projected the image of elegance and pleasure to be derived from smoking. Although the Netherlands did not exceed other European countries in tobacco consumption, one Dutch manufacturer was Europe's master at advertising and packaging. As it did for coffees and teas, Van Nelle produced some of the most memorable promotions for tobacco products. From shiny enamel street signs to lavish counter displays, from startling posters to common café checks and receipts, Van Nelle used the most contemporary styles in the most inventive, eye-catching displays to plaster its name throughout Holland. Whether by accident or design, and without ever even showing a cigarette or a person smoking it, Van Nelle imbued its products with an unforgettable aura of sophistication.

410

VAN NELLE'S TABAK!
Enamel sign, 1925
Jac. Jongert

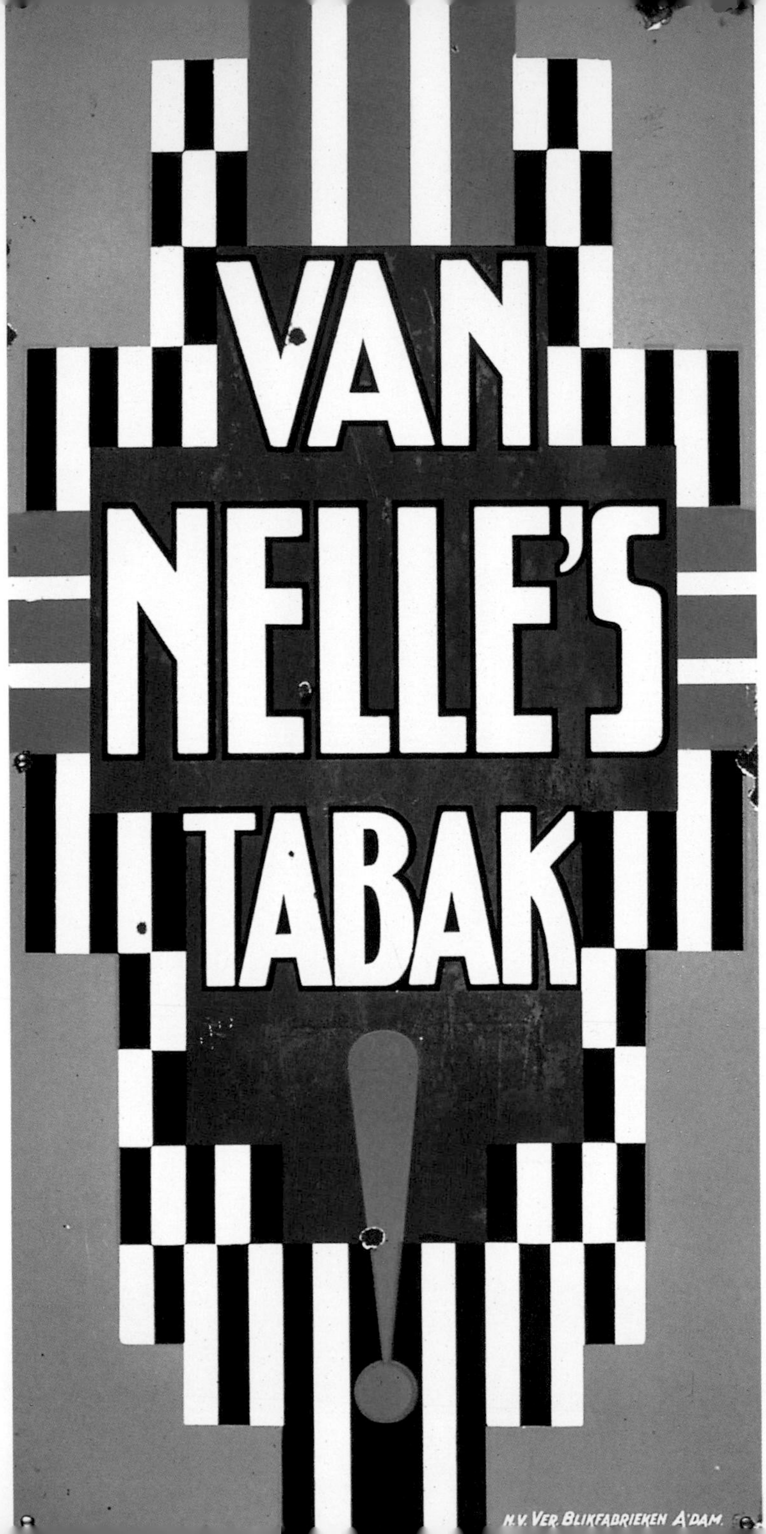

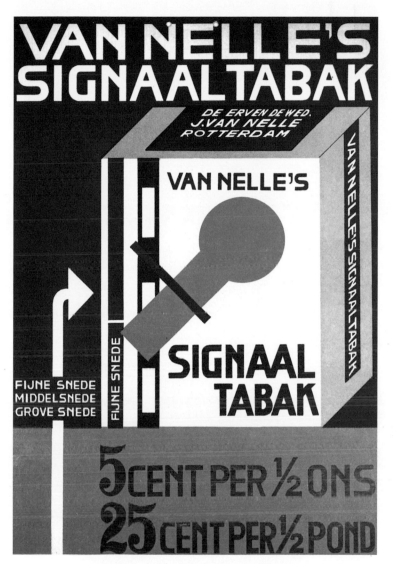

VAN NELLE'S SIGNAAL TABAK
Tabacco advertisement, 1927
Jac. Jongert

VAN NELLE'S TABAK
Restaurant check, c. 1926
Jac. Jongert

DUIS
SIGAREN
TABAK
SIGARETTEN

PHILIPS
Cigarette trademark, 1922

SPOORTABAK
Cigarette trademark, 1927

THE RENAISSANCE OF DUTCH TYPOGRAPHY IN THE EARLY TWENTIETH CENTURY SPRANG FROM BOTH THE RESURGENCE OF TRADITIONAL FORMS AND THE DEVELOPMENT OF AVANT-GARDE APPROACHES. THE TRADITIONALISTS BELIEVED THAT THE MOST FUNCTIONAL TYPOGRAPHY WAS ELEGANT **TYPOGRAPHY** AND "INVISIBLE." THEY REEVALUATED TYPOGRAPHIC STANDARDS WITH THE PRIMARY GOAL OF PROVIDING THE WRITER WITH THE TOOLS OF COMMUNICATION. THE AVANT-GARDE BELIEVED THAT TYPE HAD AN AUTONOMOUS FUNCTION, AND THEY USED ALL AVAILABLE MEANS TO EMPHASIZE "EXPRESSIVE, ASSOCIATIVE, AND PLASTIC POSSIBILITIES WITH THE FORMS OF LETTERS THEMSELVES" (KEES BOOS, IN FRIEDMAN, 1982). THE TRADITIONALISTS REESTABLISHED ORDER AND CREATED A NEED FOR SERIOUS TYPOGRAPHERS IN A FIELD DEBASED BY POOR AESTHETICS; THE MODERNISTS TESTED THE LIMITS OF TYPOGRAPHIC EXPRESSION AND PUSHED THE BOUNDARIES OF PLASTIC FORM. TUCKED BETWEEN THE TWO EXTREMES WAS AN ECLECTIC MANNER USED BY THE MAJORITY OF DUTCH BUSINESSES FOR ADVERTISING AND LOGOS. SOME TYPOGRAPHIC INNOVATIONS WERE INFLUENCED BY THE TWO FORMAL SCHOOLS, BUT MOST WERE UNTHEORETICAL SOLUTIONS TO COMMERCIAL PROBLEMS. THE LETTERING RANGED FROM THE UNREPENTANTLY OLD-FASHIONED TO THE PROUDLY EXPRESSIONISTIC. OF THESE, THE ONES THAT WERE DISTINCTLY DUTCH EVOLVED FROM WENDINGEN STYLE DECORATIVISM.

VAN NELLE'S
PRISMA
THEE

Germania

No. 6 • 6e JAARGANG
• MAART 1936 •

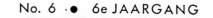

DE PROLETARISCHE VROUW

BLAD VOOR ARBEIDSTERS EN ARBEIDERSVROUWEN, WEEKBLAD VAN DEN BOND VAN SOC·DEM·VROUWEN·PROPAGANDA·CLUBS IN NEDERLAND
ONDER REDACTIE VAN C. POTHUIS·SMIT

GEÏLLUSTREERD SCHILDERSBLAD
UITGAVE DRUKKERIJ EISMA LEEUWARDEN

GERMANIA
Masthead for sports magazine, 1936

DE PROLETARISCHE
VROUW
Masthead for working women's
newspaper, 1929

GEÏLLUSTREERD
SCHILDERSBLAD
Masthead for housepainters'
magazine, 1940

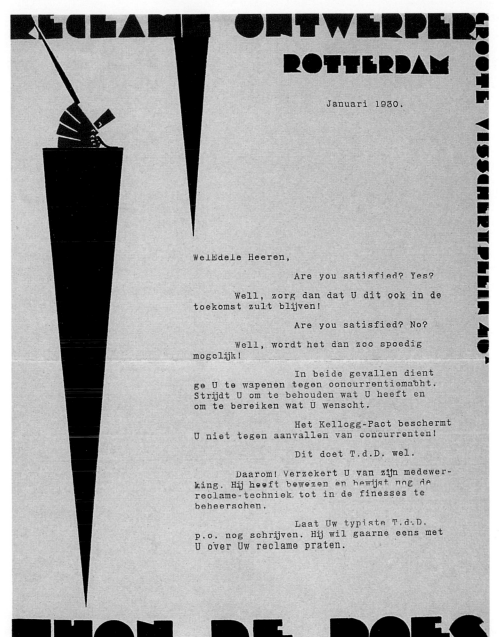

RECLAME
ONTWERPER
Designer's stationery,
1930
Thon de Does

LICONA

LICONA
Fabric trademark, 1929

PERLA

PERLA
Soap trademark, 1929

PERPLEX

PERPLEX
Carpenter's trademark, 1930

P. VAN BERKEL LTD.
Meat advertisement, c. 1925
Paul Schuitema

SUPERIOR
DUTCH
HAM
BONELESS

P van BERKEL LTD
ROTTERDAM
HOLLAND

A REAL LUXURY

BRI
MOD

TISH
ISH
ERN

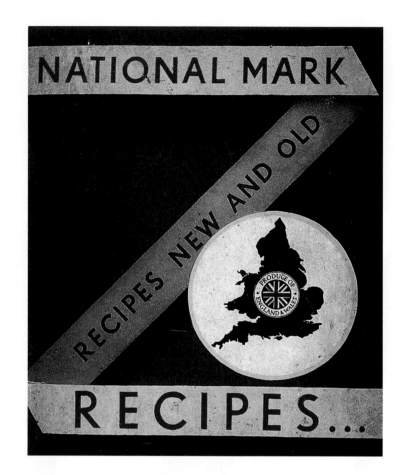

petition abroad. Much was written in the design trade journals about marshaling progressive graphic

design to combat this threat, particularly the resurgence of German trade in the post-war era. Despite

the fact that the devastation of World War I had temporarily paralyzed German industry, an editorial in

a 1924 issue of England's *Commercial Art* magazine anticipated its inevitable recovery and ensuing

competition. Germany was in the midst of a tremendous spiritual awakening, warned the editorial:

"... German laboratories and art centers are enthusiastic and active and preparing for the day of recov-

ery." Against this fervent German impulse the commercial art movement in England was unimpressive.

So the editorial further cautioned: "It behooves us to emulate the Germans in the attention they pay to laboratory and studio work, for only by these means will we be able to keep pace with our rivals ..."

The critics of stodgy British advertising also saw America as a worthy opponent: "Why is it that our standard of commercial art does not approach that of the Americans," asked Brian Rowe in "Commercial Art in England and America: A Difference in Attitude" (*Commercial Art*, 1924). He blamed it in part on the nonexistence in England of "a breed of men called art directors," which he described as Renaissance men of advertising who controlled both image and text to accomplish a creative end. But despite his awe of American practice, Rowe concluded that "We can show them infinitely more progress since the war than they have made .... We can show them ... modernity [that] they have not the wit or courage to use."

Rowe sounded a clarion call for members of a new generation of "modern artists for industry," including Austin Cooper, Tom Purvis, and the American expatriate Edward McKnight Kauffer, who in the face of prevailing conservatism produced sophisticated—and progressive—graphic design that was wedded to the avant-garde languages of Cubism, Futurism, and Vorticism. Through their efforts modernism gradually found a niche. Outlets for this work became more common. Each of these artists, in fact, was the beneficiary of a far-sighted patron, Frank Pick, who from 1908 to 1940 directed publicity respectively for the Underground and London Passenger Transport Board. In the early teens he was instrumental in developing an identity and publicity campaign for The Underground, which evolved into the British poster renaissance of the late 1920s. Pick reasoned that to entice its passengers the Underground and its bus service not only had to provide clean, comfortable, and efficient transport, it had to promote its services in an artistic manner—even the maps required a creative touch. Pick's poster campaign gave the people of London a virtual picture gallery, which John Harrison in *Posters and Publicity: Fine Printing and Design* (The Studio, Ltd., 1927) proclaimed was "[A]s fine in some ways it seems to me as the Tate or the National [Galleries] and with much more imposing numbers of visitors." He continued by saying that Pick "has made possible by enlightened patronage the admirable work of the modernist advertising designers who would otherwise have starved."

By the mid-1920s the Underground, British Railway, and English travel posters in general began winning recognition in international advertising competitions and exhibitions. Upon the heels of this success the trade journals were quick to announce that "England was leading the way." But as if to qualify their approbatory articles, many stated that the new generation of posters and advertisements were characterized by a "style of refined modernism" wherein the lettering is "effective without being eccentric." Despite the apparent popular approval of avant-gardisms born of European art movements, the design critics believed that strict British composure had to be maintained.

One critic described the new British accent in graphic design as "old English-modernism." He was referring to how British taste had adapted to the new visual vocabulary and reconciled itself to what he referred to as "conflicting emotions aroused by modern art." These debates centered around the triumph of beauty over ugliness and, more importantly, national pride over international assimilation. Germany was the "inspirational country of modernism and they show very clearly how the grotesque may very easily degenerate into the merely unpleasant," argued an editorial in *Commercial Art* (1918). Under no circumstances did English critics want to succumb to foreign design domination, especially by their former enemy. But the *Commercial Art* editorial did acknowledge the reason for England's gradual adoption of what had become an international style: "The wireless and Cook's Tours have produced an extraordinary similarity between us all, and there is little to distinguish one capital from another, except language. We in England cannot afford to ignore what other people are doing unless we want our trade to go the way of our sport championships."

A fragile trade balance ultimately dictated the look of advertising art. And it was the job of England's agencies (or art departments for industry) to put modernism to effective use. Among the most prominent firms were the Carlton Studios, the Basset Gray Studios, the Crichton Studios, and the Clement Dane Studios. But of them all, Crawford's was the top agency and a leading proponent of pictorial modernism. Ashley Havinden (known as Ashley) was one of Crawford's most accomplished staff designers, who through his newspaper ads and posters helped define English graphic modernity. "...[I]n Ashley's work there is a feeling of newness hard to define," wrote poster artist Horace Taylor in *Commercial Art* (1932). "He does not seem to be so much concerned with making his space look dignified or distinguished as with getting the advertisement read." With this in mind, Ashley introduced novel typefaces that embodied the modern spirit (and that were always associated with Crawford's), including Maximilian, Neuland, and Semisat. He often set the lettering in a swerve on a curve, which helped bust the timeworn tenet of maintaining central axis composition. Taylor noted that "the pull of these advertisements is flatteringly indicated by the vast number of imitators."

The critical mass of modern designers and new outlets got the public used to the new design. But the 1927 Advertising Exhibition held at Olympia was truly the turning point. As if to make up for England's pitiful showing at the 1925 Paris exposition, this massive undertaking, organized by the Advertising Association, was an exuberant celebration of modern and modernistic graphic techniques. The huge exhibit hall was a veritable carnival of modernistic displays. And advertisers who were still

C U L T U R E

The Vorticist group of painters, led by Wyndham Lewis, is often thought of as Britain's only original fine art movement of the twentieth century. As unique as it was in England, it was decidedly influenced by, if not a pale imitation of, French Cubism and Italian Futurism. But it was nevertheless the touchstone for a few of Britain's modern poster artists of the early 1920s. The most renowned of these was responsible for a large number of the cultural posters (as well as other genres) preserved today. E. McKnight Kauffer, an American expatriot who came to England as a painter and became a leading commercial artist, contributed to and created public taste instead of merely following it. "There is nothing popular in the ordinary sense about Kauffer's work," wrote John Harrison in *Posters and Publicity: Fine Printing and Design* (1927). "It is abstract and advanced. Yet public interest has been roused to a great degree. Mr. Kauffer rivals the best of the Continental commercial designers. He is not, however, specifically English in quality." Kauffer's work was a synthesis of European modern artistic inventions—collage, montage, flat color fields, layered transparencies, and more. But his work, which was ubiquitous in England between 1919 and 1939, was a measure of the British visual culture of the era. Of course he was not alone in creating publicity for cultural events, but in this chapter it is clear that his contributions creatively far outdistanced the other artists who relied on spruced up traditional narratives. Kauffer's typography and imagery were modern to a fault. In the cultural arena—particularly with publicity for arts and architecture events—Kauffer's cubistic method was well suited and received. But not all cultural happenings were as avant-garde as these. So an equal number of the works in this chapter represent a populist culture, cabaret, or music hall experience.

THE WAY OF THE SUN

THE WAY
OF THE SUN
CATALOG
COVER, C. 1930
ARTIST
UNKNOWN

ARTS AND
CRAFTS
MAGAZINE
COVER, 1929
ARTIST:
E. MCKNIGHT
KAUFFER

ARTS AND CRAFTS

VOLUME III
NUMBER TWO
NEW SERIES
JULY 1929

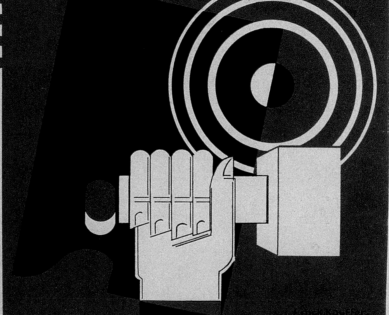

CONTENTS

THE ULTIMATE SOUND FILMS : CONTEMP-ORARY INTERIOR DE-CORATION : STATUES, MR. EPSTEIN, AND THE PUBLIC : PRESENT DAY DESIGN IN FRANCE : THE ARTS AND CRAFTS OF CANADA : THE SECRET OF MODERN ARCHITECTURE : CRIT-ICISM AND APPLIED ART : MODERN OFFICE FURNITURE : JOURNAL-ISM AND ART : MALAY ARTS AND CRAFTS : OLD IRISH GLASS : DIVERTIMENTI : ETC.

A REVIEW OF
MODERN TASTE

PRICE
ONE
SHILLING

THE RAG RAG

MAGAZINE COVER, 1929

ARTIST: HAGENDORN

THE RAG RAG

MAGAZINE COVER, 1932

ARTIST: W. E. D.

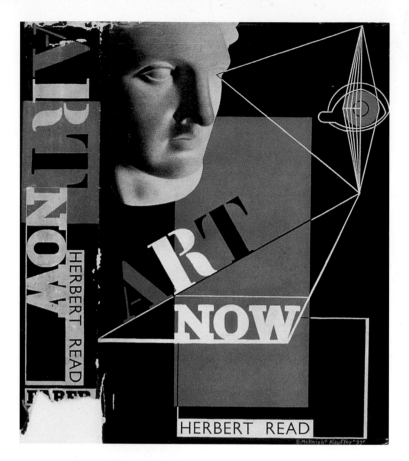

ART NOW

BOOK JACKET, 1933

ARTIST: E. MCKNIGHT KAUFFER

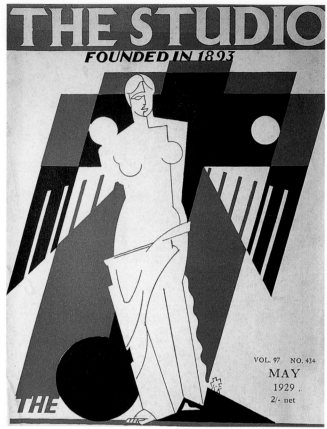

THE STUDIO

MAGAZINE COVER, 1929

ARTIST: E. MCKNIGHT KAUFFER

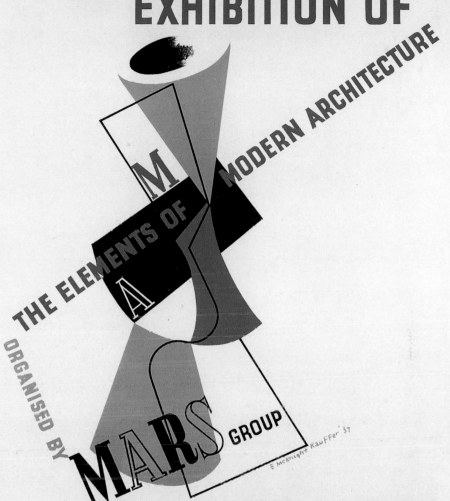

NEW ARCHITECTURE
EXHIBITION OF

THE ELEMENTS OF MODERN ARCHITECTURE

ORGANISED BY MARS GROUP

NEW BURLINGTON GALLERIES

BURLINGTON GARDENS W I

JANUARY 12TH TO 29TH 1938

10 A.M. TO 8 P.M. ADMISSION 1/-

NEW
ARCHITECTURE
POSTER,
(SIGNED) 1937
ARTIST:
E. MCKNIGHT
KAUFFER

COMMUNICATION

If modernism equals progress and progress equals communication, then modernism equals communication. Therefore, it is no surprise that modern design had an early foothold in the publicity for the English communications industry, specifically radio, telegraph, and newspapers. Perhaps the first sign of modernism was a 1919 poster by E. McKnight Kauffer for the *Daily Herald* entitled "Soaring To Success! The Early Bird," based on an earlier print titled "Flight" (1916), which was also the first cubistic advertising poster in England. This otherwise innocuous picture of birds on the wing was raised to a modernist icon by the stark, schematic rendering of the birds against a flat yellow background, which was indeed unusual for its time. From that moment it was common to see avant-gardisms that symbolized machine age progress in posters and ads. The BBC (British Broadcasting Company) was an early proponent of modernism, hiring Kauffer, among others, to contribute artwork to its growing number of program guides. But it was *Radio Times* magazine that produced the most consistently modern artworks, mostly for its covers. Here modernism was a house style influenced both by the avant-garde arts (Cubism, Vorticism, Constructivism) and the leading progressive commercial artists, including France's A. M. Cassandre (see page 73). These covers used reductive forms and essential geometries, as well as decorative and representational imagery. The airbrush had been christened the machine age artist's tool, and so a fair number of designs promoting communication were rendered with streamlined tonality and kinetic linearity. In the wake of modernism there was a lot of pseudo-modern design produced by, as one critic described it, "the smart-aleck who can always turn on a bit of modern stuff, if you want it." But that was inevitable.

THE NEW
DAILY HERALD
POSTER, C. 1930
ARTIST UNKNOWN

THE NEW DAILY HERALD
POSTER, C. 1930
ARTIST: HORACE TAYLOR

THE DAILY HERALD
POSTER, C. 1928
ARTIST: GRIMMOND

ULTRA

BROCHURE, C. 1928

ARTIST UNKNOWN

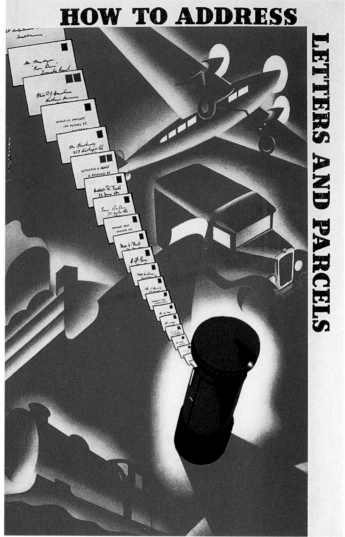

HOW TO ADDRESS

BROCHURE, C. 1928

ARTIST UNKNOWN

SPEED YOUR
MESSAGE
POSTER, 1931
ARTIST: HALLIWELL

F A S H I O N

The promotion of fashion was well served by the Art Deco style. Haute couture and daily dress were mythologized through simplified representations of the human form set against modernistic backdrops. In England this publicity was influenced by modern French and German mannerisms—the former, cubistic renderings of men and women; the latter, reductive, essential outlines and color fields. Tom Purvis masterfully adapted the German "sachplakat" (object poster) method in his images for Austin Reed's, England's quality men's clothier. Purvis's male figures were monumental yet also identified with the average consumer. Most women, on the other hand, were rendered inertly as if they were robots, prompting Lucy B. Kitchin to write in *Advertising Display* (January, 1929) a critique entitled "Why Not A Natural Woman?" She was referring to the proliferation of "the Puppet Lady." This mannerism, which is the emblem of the moderne female, was started by the fashion artists who, as Kitchin argued, "did not want to spend too long over the portrayal of the woman wearing the dress that had to be shown, but because no two editors had the same ideal of a beautiful woman, they all disagreed heartily and heatedly …" The vogue swung from the ultra-realistic drawing to stylized design void of individual characteristics. "The evolution of this woman," continued Kitchin, "could be shown as the 'Smart Woman' in so many countries …. But in losing nationality she lost also her individuality, and for this reason she is in danger of losing her being." Apparently there was another reason for this trend. "So little artistic ability is required on the part of those who perpetrate these things," wrote one store's advertising manager in *Advertising Display*, "that they naturally do not cost nearly as much as good artistic drawings do. This alone is sufficient recommendation to endow them with eternal life.…"

RIGHT:

AUSTIN REED'S

POSTER, 1927

ARTIST: TOM PURVIS

BELOW:

AUSTIN REED'S

POSTER, 1928

ARTIST: AUSTIN COOPER

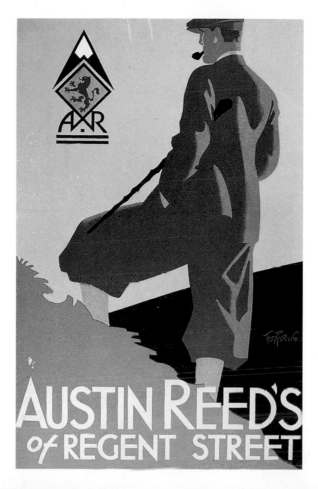

AUX ÉLÉGANTES

ADVERTISEMENT, 1923

ARTIST: ALDO COSOMATIC

VIGIL

POSTER, 1925

ARTIST UNKNOWN

FLANNELS

POSTER, C. 1928

ARTIST UNKNOWN

WOLSEY

ADVERTISEMENT, 1930

ARTIST UNKNOWN

WON'T SHRINK

POSTER, C. 1927

ARTIST: AUBREY HAMMOND

WON'T FADE

POSTER, C. 1927

ARTIST: AUBREY HAMMOND

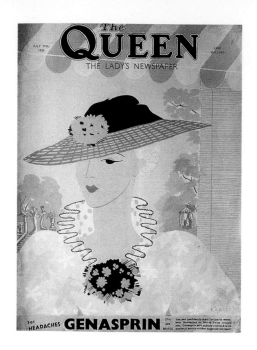

THE QUEEN

MAGAZINE COVER, 1935

ARTIST: KARAS

LONDON

MAGAZINE COVER, C. 1932

ARTIST: WILTON WILLIAMS

THE QUEEN

MAGAZINE COVER, 1935

ARTIST: KARAS

UNTITLED

SHIRT BOX, C. 1930

ARTIST UNKNOWN

456

WEAR A KESTOS BRASSIÈRE
WHEN YOU BATHE

The quite perfect bathing costumes of to-day, which so light-heartedly challenge attention, need the subtle flattering finish that only a Kestos Brassière with its unique crossway pull and uplift can provide, to enable them to be worn with that air of nonchalance which is so captivating.

To look your best always wear a Kestos Brassière when you bathe. In seven sizes, prices 3/11 to 22/6. Sold everywhere.

Catalogue on request.

KESTOS LTD., HADDOK HOUSE
REGENT STREET, LONDON, W.1
(Wholesale only).

KESTOS Décolleté

KESTOS BRASSIÈRE

KESTOS

ADVERTISEMENT, 1932

ARTIST: LEO KLIN

KESTOS

ADVERTISEMENT, 1932

ARTIST: LEO KLIN

UNDERGROUND

Modern English graphic design began underground and surged upward. Posters for the London Underground, which advertised its services as well as scenic sights occurring within range of its lines and stations, evolved under the direction of Frank Pick from prosaic landscapes to stylized abstractions. Pick had a vision of a better urban environment and was determined to use his position as director of publicity to educate and raise the public's standard of taste. The posters avoided the overtly hard-sell images common to most advertising in favor of subtle allusions to the advertised themes. For the most part this modern approach was popular among passengers and artists alike. "The Underground Railway is ... a tower of strength to the case of artistic advertising," wrote John Harrison in *Posters and Publicity: Fine Printing and Design* (1927). But some critics nevertheless argued against the viability of modern art: "By all means try and educate the public taste," wrote G.W. Duncan in *Penrose Annual* (1935), "but do not use commercial posters simply as an indirect form of publicity for artists and art galleries." Yet critiques of the Underground's modernism paled next to the actual results. The posters strikingly illustrated London's beauty spots and maintained an unceasing flow of unique and amusing designs by the most capable artists of the day. The Underground was, moreover, a pioneer of integrated design strategies. In addition to posters, Pick commissioned Edward Johnston to design a block-letter alphabet exclusively used for station signs and notices that exerted an immense influence on all modern English type design. Pick also asked Johnston to design the Underground's bullseye (or red-ring) logo. It was inspired by the YMCA triangle—"only more balanced," according to Pick. The mark, found on all the Underground posters, is still used today.

THANKS TO
THE UNDERGROUND

POSTER, 1935

ARTIST: ZERO

(HANS SCHLEGER)

WINTER SALES

POSTER, 1924

ARTIST: E. MCKNIGHT

KAUFFER

LONDON'S UMBRELLA

POSTER, 1925

ARTIST: F. C. HERRICK

KEEP PACE WITH TIME

POSTER, 1927

ARTIST: F. C. HERRICK

FROM WINTERS GLOOM...

POSTER, 1927

ARTIST. E. MCKNIGHT KAUFFER

COME OUT OF DOORS

POSTER, 1928

ARTIST: ALMA FAULKNER

SHOP BETWEEN 10 AND 4 THE QUIET HOURS AND BY UNDERGROUND

A MAIN LINE
STATION

MAY 1923

Sanders Phillips and Co., Ltd., THE BAYNARD PRESS, Chryssell Road, S.W.9.

WHAT A SYSTEM OF
BUS ROUTES MEANS?
720 BUSES ARE WANTED
TO WORK THIS NETWORK
OF 21 SERVICES

POWER

POSTER, 1931

ARTIST: F. MCKNIGHT

KAUFFER

A TRAIN EVERY

90 SECONDS

POSTER, C. 1937

ARTIST: ABRAM GAMES

SPEED

POSTER, 1930

ARTIST: ALAN ROGERS

BRITISH
INDUSTRIES FAIR
POSTER, 1928
ARTIST: E. MCKNIGHT KAUFFER

THE MOTOR
SHOW OLYMPIA
POSTER, 1928
ARTIST: ERIC FRASER

MOTOR SHOW
POSTER, 1928
ARTIST: HERRY PERRY

OLYMPIA MOTOR SHOW

POSTER, 1932

ARTIST UNKNOWN

INDUSTRY

Unlike France, Germany, and Russia, to name a few industrialized nations that embraced artists, English industry was not always a willing recipient of art in the service of commerce. While industrial leaders more or less understood the value of advertising to promote their wares to the masses, they saw it as being rather straightforward and not to be mucked about by modern design. Some industrial leaders and advertising critics looked upon the conceits of modern designers as distracting from the job at hand—to sell the goods. "In the majority of British industries today," wrote W. D. H. McCullough in *Commercial Art and Industry* (1931), "the accountant and the engineer have far too much say, and the artist has far too little." Industry paid lip service to artists whom McCullough describes as having been "snatched from Chelsea and dumped into enormous factories in the North Country, where they have been set down in dank and gloomy offices and told to be artistic." Change began to take place when it was pointed out that once again the Germans were taking the lead in the areas of both industrial and advertising design. British industry gradually came around to accepting modernism as a code for progress. The creation of Art Departments for Industry in the early 1930s had a lot to do with a fundamental change in attitude, as did the artistic and creative advisors who insinuated themselves in corporate decisions. On the government side, by 1932 in London both the Board of Trade and the Board of Education established a departmental committee to deal with art and industry (later to be known as the British Arts Council). The goal of the committee was to develop in London a standing exhibition of good design and current manufacture and to organize local and traveling exhibitions. In turn these exhibits (including fairs devoted to advertising) influenced the nature of industrial design throughout the 1930s.

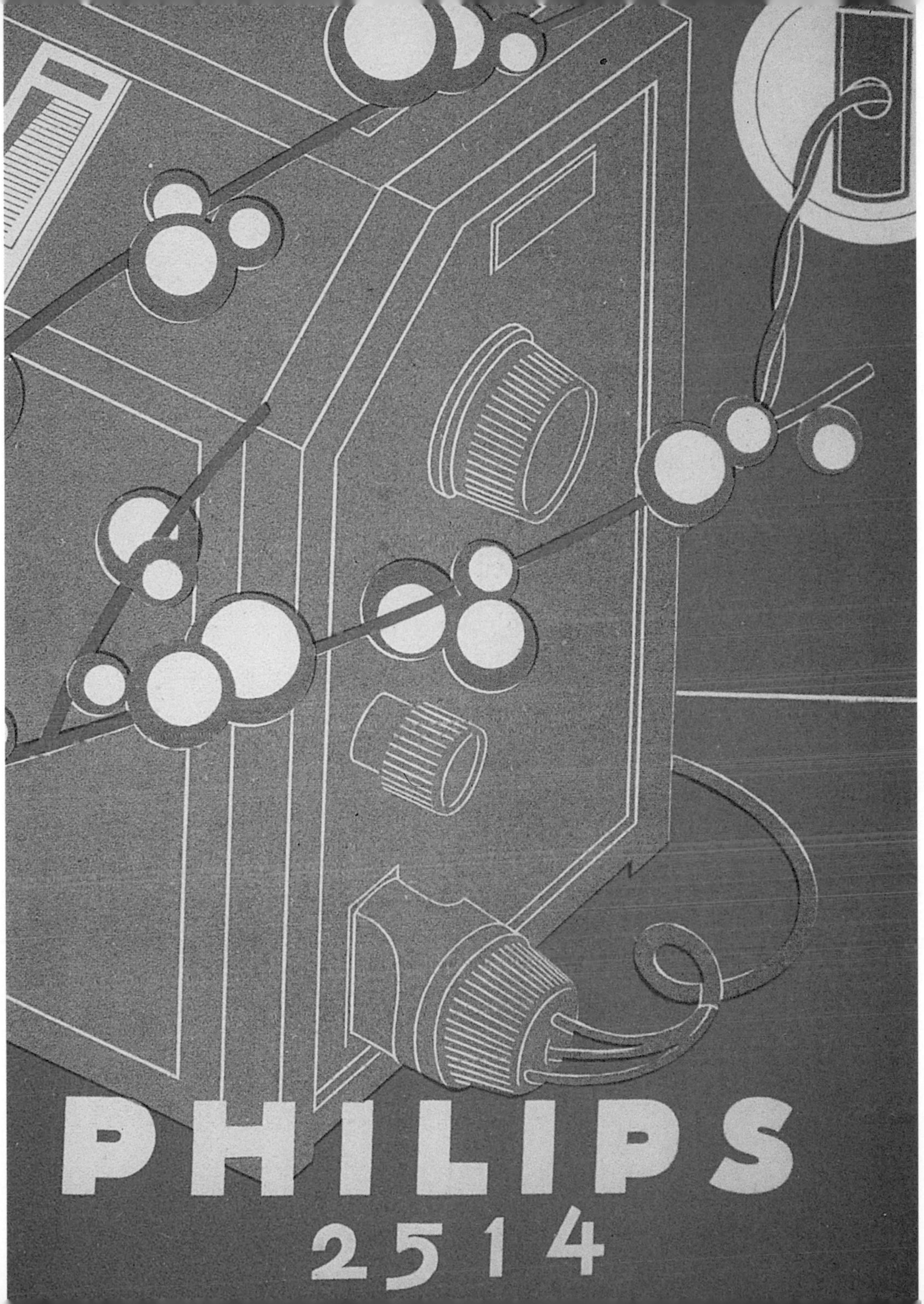

PHILIPS
POSTER, C. 1932
ARTIST UNKNOWN

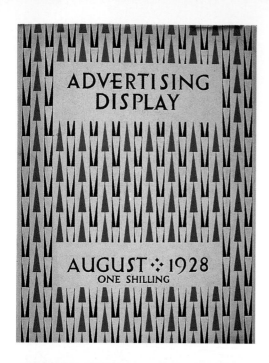

ADVERTISING DISPLAY

MAGAZINE COVER, 1928

ARTIST UNKNOWN

ADVERTISING DISPLAY

MAGAZINE COVER, 1928

ARTIST: E. McKNIGHT KAUFFER

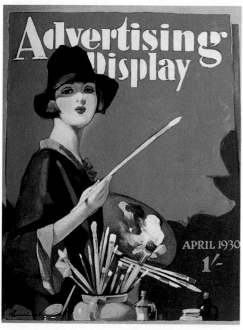

ADVERTISING DISPLAY

MAGAZINE COVER, 1930

ARTIST: BARRIBAL

ADVERTISING DISPLAY

MAGAZINE COVER, 1929

ARTIST UNKNOWN

PATHÉ 95
POSTER, 1928
ARTIST UNKNOWN

THE YEAR BOOK
BOOK COVER, 1929
ARTISTS: WALLACE & TIERNAN

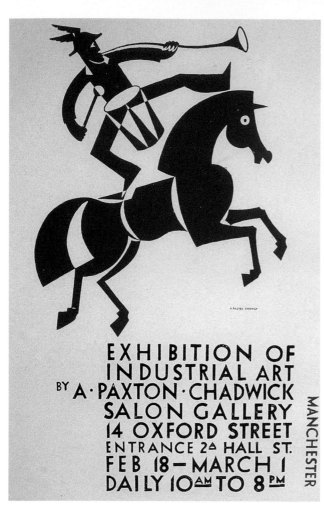

EXHIBITION OF
INDUSTRIAL ART
BY A·PAXTON·CHADWICK
SALON GALLERY
14 OXFORD STREET
ENTRANCE 2ᴬ HALL ST.
FEB 18 — MARCH 1
DAILY 10ᴬᴹ TO 8ᴾᴹ

MANCHESTER

**EXHIBITION OF
INDUSTRIAL ART**
POSTER, C. 1928
ARTIST: A. PAXTON
CHADWICK

ADVERTISING
WORLD
Souvenir of the
Advertising Exhibition
AUGUST 1927   PRICE 2/-

ADVERISING WORLD
MAGAZINE COVER, 1927
ARTIST: F. HINDLE

NOBEL
POSTER, 1924
ARTIST UNKNOWN

BRITISCHE
INDUSTRIEMESSE
POSTER, 1938
ARTIST: TOM PURVIS

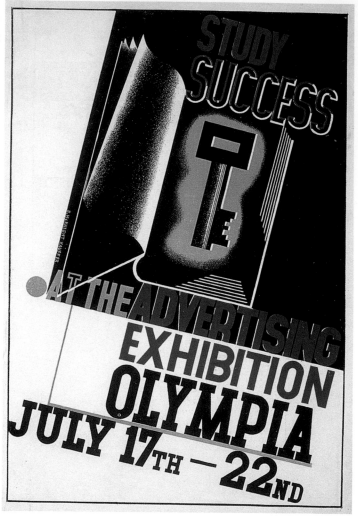

EXHIBITION OLYMPIA
CATALOG COVER, 1927
ARTIST: E. MCKNIGHT
KAUFFER

JUNE 20-JULY 12

B A

EXHIBITION OF
BRITISH INDUSTRIAL
ART IN THE HOME
LONDON
DORLAND HALL·LOWER REGENT ST.

BIA
POSTER, C. 1928
ARTIST:
AUSTIN COOPER

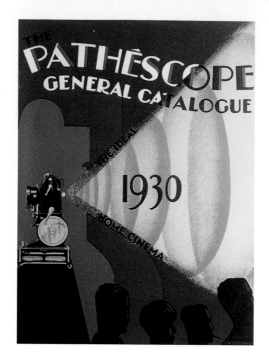

PATHÉSCOPE

CATALOG COVER, 1930

ARTIST: V. L. NANVERS

AGFA

POSTER, C. 1934

ARTIST UNKNOWN

SELO

POSTER, C. 1938

ARTIST UNKNOWN

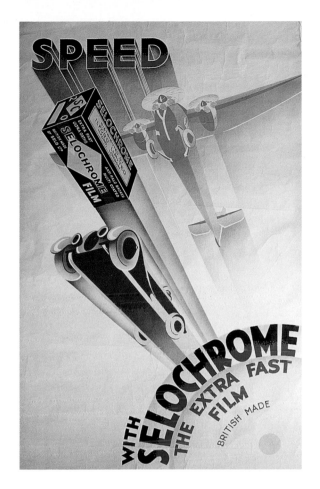

SELOCHROME

ADVERTISEMENT, C. 1938

ARTIST UNKNOWN

LUKOS

PACKAGE, C. 1938

ARTIST UNKNOWN

SELO

ADVERTISEMENT, C. 1935

ARTIST UNKNOWN

S U n D R I E S

Compared to France's exuberance and Germany's polish, England's package designs for sundries were not really very good. "This is a form of advertising we should do well to develop as the Empire Marketing Board is trying to develop it in connection with its general imperial scheme," wrote Joseph Thorp in *Design in Modern Printing: The Year Book of the Design and Industries Association 1927–28.* "We are a nation of exporters, and it is of primary importance for us to make our goods attractive from the point of view of their ultimate consumers and not from our own .... We must now make a closer study of taste, remembering that attractive packaging is a strong sales asset." Yet it took some time before this particular design form caught up with the rest of the world's standards. Which is curious, since advertising for sundries—those ubiquitous displays strategically positioned on pharmacy counter-tops—was certainly on a par with other nations' achievements. The fact was that the English consumers preferred packages that spoke of tradition. Heraldic decoration and ye olde English ornament were apparently more successful lures than the moderne filigree common to this kind of product. Moreover, England did not have as thriving a cosmetic and toiletry industry as France or Italy (where packages were also quite good). The most popular perfumes were imported from the continent, while fine English-made beauty products were hard to obtain. Given design virtue alone, only razor blade packages stand above the rest. These superb examples of anonymous Lilliputian graphic art made the most of a confined image area, and when seen together (pages 484-485), they become a veritable specimen sheet of eccentric moderne typography. Otherwise the examples in this chapter appear to be only reluctantly modern and a few are stubbornly mainstream.

KHASANA
COUNTER
DISPLAY,
C. 1930
ARTIST
UNKNOWN

KHASANA
BLUSHCREAM & LIPSTICK
KISS AND
WATERPROOF

BLUSH • CORAL • CARMINE

BRISTOW'S

COUNTER DISPLAY,

C. 1925

ARTIST UNKNOWN

TRAVELETTE

PACKAGE, C. 1925

ARTIST UNKNOWN

HANDY PACK

TIN, C. 1925

ARTIST UNKNOWN

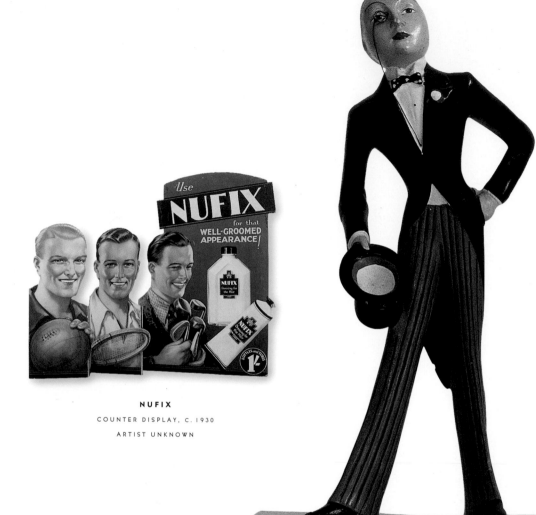

NUFIX
COUNTER DISPLAY, C. 1930
ARTIST UNKNOWN

ROLLS RAZOR
COUNTER DISPLAY, C. 1928
ARTIST UNKNOWN

MELTONIAN
COUNTER DISPLAY,
C. 1930
ARTIST UNKNOWN

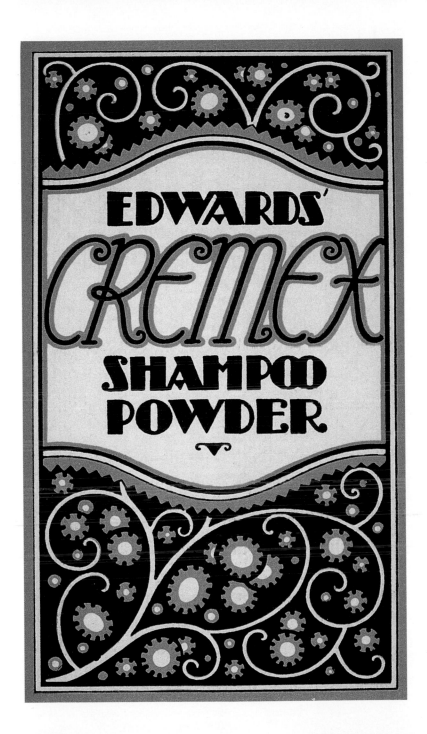

CREMEX

LABEL, 1921

ARTIST: A. ERDMANN

STA-RITE

PACKAGE, C. 1927

ARTIST UNKNOWN

BŪTYWAVE

COUNTER DISPLAY, 1928

ARTIST UNKNOWN

BLUE Gillette REGD TRADE MARK BLADE

King Gillette

Gillette

REGD TRADE MARK

ELECTRICALLY TEMPERED

1/3 FOR FIVE

BLUE GILLETTES

ATTA·BOY

ATTA·BOY RAZOR-BLADE

RAZOR BLADE

ASSORTED
RAZOR BLADES
1930—1939
ARTISTS UNKNOWN

BLUE GILLETTES
COUNTER DISPLAY,
C. 1933
ARTIST UNKNOWN

The Dandy (REGTD)

THE DANDY
THE DANDY

EXACTA
RAZOR BLADE

EXACTA
RAZOR BLADES

ASSORTED RAZOR BLADES

1930—1939

ARTISTS UNKNOWN

Food, dri

commodi

rior pack

was paid

assuming

of brash

worship t

new like

average

were first

with entre

this style

popular a

Saxon Mil

an advert

With ever

mold) the

eral. And

incorporat

BIRD'S CUSTARD
ADVERTISEMENT, C. 1928
ARTIST UNKNOWN

BIRD'S CUSTARD
ADVERTISEMENT, C. 1928
ARTIST UNKNOWN

ENO'S
POSTER, 1924
ARTIST: E. MCKNIGHT KAUFFER

"OXO"
TIN, C. 1930
ARTIST UNKNOWN

BASS

SIGN, C. 1930

ARTIST UNKNOWN

SCHWEPPES

ADVERTISEMENT, 1926

ARTIST: F. S. MAY

SEAGERS

ADVERTISEMENT, C. 1928

ARTIST UNKNOWN

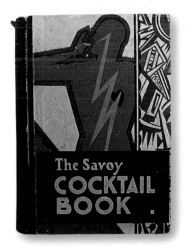

**THE SAVOY
COCKTAIL BOOK**

BOOK COVER, 1930

ARTIST: GILBERT RUMBOLD

491

TYPOGRAPHY

Every nation has a national symbol; some even have their own typeface. Although not officially designated as such, two faces of the 1920s and 1930s are inextricably English. One is Edward Johnston's block letter designed for the Underground, which caused consternation among typographers when it first appeared in 1916. "It was a breathtaking surprise to nearly all who could be interested," wrote Noel Rooke (quoted in *Edward Johnston* by Priscilla Johnston, Pentalic Corporation, NY, 1976), "the very lowest category of letter had been suddenly lifted to a place among the highest." The other was the sans-serif caps designed in 1928 by Eric Gill. Originally Johnston and Gill were hired to work together on the Underground face. Gill dropped out only to revisit the modern sans-serif years later when he was commissioned by Lanston Monotype Coporation to create a new alphabet. Gill's type caused a "storm of excitement," according to Beatrice Warde in *Advertising Display* (1928), because gothics belonged to an "abhorred family of type." The precisionist quality of Gill Sans challenged the archaism of most diehard traditionalists. Nevertheless, English typography critics warned against novelty for its own sake: "Our job in letter designing is not to give free reins to our invention, but to keep it well within the bounds of the established shapes of those signals called letters," exhorted Joseph Thorp, who attacked so-called "original" designers of type who filled the specimen books of the 1920s. He argued that originality consisted in departing as far as possible from the established convention by "the addition of nicks and bulges and slopes, the heightening or lowering of cross-strokes, the backward or forward sloping of the axis of the 'counters'—a practice developed to a distressing extent."

ENGLAND

POSTER, 1928

ARTIST:

AUSTIN COOPER

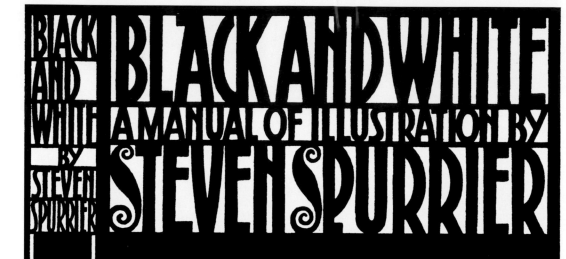

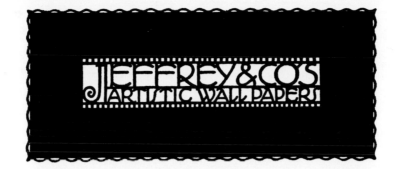

JEFFREY & CO'S
BUSINESS CARD, C. 1923
ARTIST: A. ERDMANN

EXHIBITION
ADVERTISEMENT, C. 1920
ARTIST: A. ERDMANN

OMO
LABEL, C. 1923
ARTIST: A. ERDMANN

CREDITS

With the exception of the following, all materials in this book are on loan from private collections.

FRENCH MODERN: Platkatsammlung Museum für Gestaltung Zürich: 60, 73, Wolfsonian-Florida International University: 29, 33, 77; Mirko Ili´c: 81; Posters Please Inc.: 32 (top).

ITALIAN ART DECO: Sergio Coradeschi: 106, 116–117; Ex Libris: 112–113; Centro Studio Archivio della Communicazione dell'Universita degli Studi di Parma: 121. 123; Lazzaroni & C. S.p.A.: 156; Davide Campari Milano S.p.A.: 162–165.

GERMAN MODERN: Kunstgewerbemuseum Zürich: 214 (top), 215, 217, 220, 221 (top right and left), 222 (top middle), 224, 225, 226, 227, 228, 232, 234, 235 (right), 239, 240, 244 (right), 246, 251; Wolfsonian-Florida International University:203, 208, 229; Ex Libris: 250 (bottom).

SPANISH ART DECO: Plakatsammlung Museum Für Gestaltung Zürich: 286 (lower left, upper and lower right), 287, 300; Hoover Institution Archive: 285, 286 (upper left), 288, 289, (top left, right and center), 290, 291, 292, 293 (upper right); Enric Satué: 28 (bottom), 296–297, 304 (right), 311 (top left), 312 (top), 313, 314, 317 (left), 325 (right), 332, 333 (right), 338; Chisholm Larsson Gallery: 293 (upper left, lower left, lower right), 301, 309; Arxiu Giralt-Miracle: 326 (top left and top right), 346.

DUTCH MODERN: The Schule und Museum für Gestaltung Zürich: 354, 367 (bottom left, top right), 376, 381 (right), 387, 394, 397 (top), 400, 403, 412. Wabnitz Editions: 365. Wolfsonian-Florida International University: 366, 367 (top left, bottom right), 368 (top), 377, 378, 379, 382, 383, 390, 391, 392 (top); Fairleigh Dickinson University, Friendship Library: 373; Van Sabben Poster Auctions: 368 (bottom left, bottom right), 380, 381 (left), 386 (right), 392 (bottom left, right); International Instituut voor Scoiale Geschiedenis: 369, 370, 371; The Stedelijik Museum: 384, 385 (left), 399 (left); Philips Nederland NV: 395, 396, 397 (bottom); Miscellaneous Man: 404 (middle); Douwe Egberts Van Nelle: 404 (left, right), 405, 411, 413, 417; Heineken Internationaal: 407 (top); Michael Sheehe: 419; Dick Mann: 423.

BRITISH MODERN: Robert Opie Collection: 431, 439–441, 445, 446 (bottom left and right), 447–448, 452, 454–457 469, 470 (bottom left), 471 (left), 472, 473 474 (left), 476–477, 479–482, 483 (top right), 484 (middle), 487, 488 (top left, right and middle), 489, 490, 491 (top right), 492–493, 495. Wolfsonian-Florida International University: 449; The London Transport Museum: 459–467; Plakatsammlung Museum für Gestaltung Zürich: 475; Steven Guarnaccia: 484–485.

ACKNOWLEDGMENTS

This book would not have been possible without the enthusiastic support of our current Chronicle editor, Alan Rapp. Thanks also to Chad Roberts at Louise Fili Ltd., for his attention to the design and production of this new edition. Also we are grateful to Leah Lococo and Mary Jane Callister for their respective design input to the original series. Also we are indebted to Nion McEvoy, who commissioned the first book, and to Bill LeBlond, who was our editor for most of the series.

Thanks to Jordi Duro and Sonia Biancalani Levethan our invaluable research assistants. And thanks to the following for their creative and production assistance: Michael Carabetta; Julia Flagg; Charlotte Stone; Chawa Costa; Patricia Draher; Lee Bearson; Austin Hughes; Lesley Bruynesteyn, Martine Trélaün; Sarah Putman. Here's a tip of the hat to our agent Sarah Jane Freymann. And thanks to the following for their generous cooperation and for loaning materials to individual books: James Fraser; Helga Krempke Catherine Büer, Barbar Meili, Kurt Thaler at the Museum für Gestaltung Zürich and Kunstgewerbemuseum Zürich; B. Hausmann at the Plakatsammlung Museum für Gestaltung Zürich; Kathy Leff, Anita Gross, Jim Findlay at the Wolfsonian Museum, Miami, Fla.; George Theophiles; Irving Oaklander; Karl Bernhard; Elaine Lustig Cohen; Robert Opie; Mirko Ilic; Steven Guarnaccia; Greg Leeds; Seymour Chwast; Paula Scher; Eric Baker; Erik Spiekermann; Jacqueline Eberhard at Nestlé S.A; Sophie Henley-Price at Somology Editions d'Art; Enrico Castruccio; Robert Brown of Rinehold Brown Gallery; Peter Weiss; Luigi and Paolo Lazzaroni at Lazzaroni & C; Geom. Egidio Bossetti at Davide Campario Milano; Sergio Coradeschi; Anna Maria Gandini; Prof. Eugenio Monzato at Museo Civico L. Bailoo; Franco Arduini at Biblioteca Marucelliana; Leo Lionni; Jack Banning of Ubu Gallery; Gloria Biancino at Centro Studie Archivbio della Comunicaszione dell' Univerita degli Studio di Parma; Cecilia Guidici Sevetti; Anthony Pizzuto; Chris McKee; Louise Porter; Giovanni Salviati; Matteo Tesoldi; Paola Antonelli; Paolo Guidoti; Lita Talarcio; Lucia Perucci; Emilo Duró; Enric Satué; Sonia Biancalani; Reyes Zavala; Jordi Carulla; Francesc Ribot; Carol Leadenham at the Hoover Institution Archives; Robert Chisholm at Chisholm Larsson Gallery; Gail Chisholm at Chisholm Gallery; Philip Williams at Philip Williams Gallery; David Sánchez; Albert Azuar; Ariadna Blanc; Imma Más; Daniel and Pau Giralt-Miracle; Maria Soto; Arxlu Giralt Miracle; Alicia Gomez; Lluïsa Camarero; Carme Carrello, Montserrat Álvarez; Guillermo Luca de Tena; Venanclo Ruiz Usón; Wilma Wabnitz; Monica Strauss; A.M. Daadler-Vos of the Stedelijik Museum; Rick Vermullen; Pieter Brattinga; Piet Schruders; Willem Zwaard of Jarrbeurs Utrecht; Vivan Greblo; Henk Groenhoff; Kees Broos; Werner Lowenhardt; Fjtzen Henstra; Jam Tholenaar; René Kruis; Dick Mann; Michael Valenti; Frits Knuf; Ans Huijboom of Heineken International; A.M. van Lint of Douwe Egberts van Nelle; Paul Hefting; Mieke Beumer; Giovanni Fanelli; P. Van Wijngaarden of Gemeente Rotterdam; I.J. Blanken and J.C. van den Biggelaar of Philips Nederland; and Marien van der Heide of Intertional Institute voor Sociale Geshiedenis.

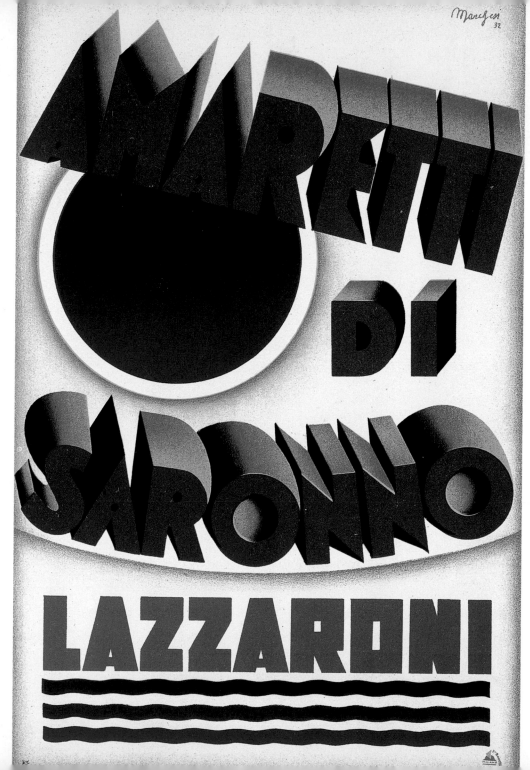